LAYERS OF LEARNING
YEAR FOUR • UNIT SIX

THE WEST
SOUTHWEST STATES
EARTH STRUCTURE
IMPRESSIONISM II

Published by HooDoo Publishing
United States of America
© 2017 Layers of Learning

(Grilled Cheese BTN Font) © Fontdiner - www.fontdiner.com
ISBN #978-1544738055

Units at a Glance: Topics For All Four Years of the Layers of Learning Program

1	History	Geography	Science	The Arts
1	Mesopotamia	Maps & Globes	Planets	Cave Paintings
2	Egypt	Map Keys	Stars	Egyptian Art
3	Europe	Global Grids	Earth & Moon	Crafts
4	Ancient Greece	Wonders	Satellites	Greek Art
5	Babylon	Mapping People	Humans in Space	Poetry
6	The Levant	Physical Earth	Laws of Motion	List Poems
7	Phoenicians	Oceans	Motion	Moral Stories
8	Assyrians	Deserts	Fluids	Rhythm
9	Persians	Arctic	Waves	Melody
10	Ancient China	Forests	Machines	Chinese Art
11	Early Japan	Mountains	States of Matter	Line & Shape
12	Arabia	Rivers & Lakes	Atoms	Color & Value
13	Ancient India	Grasslands	Elements	Texture & Form
14	Ancient Africa	Africa	Bonding	African Tales
15	First North Americans	North America	Salts	Creative Kids
16	Ancient South America	South America	Plants	South American Art
17	Celts	Europe	Flowering Plants	Jewelry
18	Roman Republic	Asia	Trees	Roman Art
19	Christianity	Australia & Oceania	Simple Plants	Instruments
20	Roman Empire	You Explore	Fungi	Composing Music

2	History	Geography	Science	The Arts
1	Byzantines	Turkey	Climate & Seasons	Byzantine Art
2	Barbarians	Ireland	Forecasting	Illumination
3	Islam	Arabian Peninsula	Clouds & Precipitation	Creative Kids
4	Vikings	Norway	Special Effects	Viking Art
5	Anglo Saxons	Britain	Wild Weather	King Arthur Tales
6	Charlemagne	France	Cells & DNA	Carolingian Art
7	Normans	Nigeria	Skeletons	Canterbury Tales
8	Feudal System	Germany	Muscles, Skin, Cardio	Gothic Art
9	Crusades	Balkans	Digestive & Senses	Religious Art
10	Burgundy, Venice, Spain	Switzerland	Nerves	Oil Paints
11	Wars of the Roses	Russia	Health	Minstrels & Plays
12	Eastern Europe	Hungary	Metals	Printmaking
13	African Kingdoms	Mali	Carbon Chemistry	Textiles
14	Asian Kingdoms	Southeast Asia	Non-metals	Vivid Language
15	Mongols	Caucasus	Gases	Fun With Poetry
16	Medieval China & Japan	China	Electricity	Asian Arts
17	Pacific Peoples	Micronesia	Circuits	Arts of the Islands
18	American Peoples	Canada	Technology	Indian Legends
19	The Renaissance	Italy	Magnetism	Renaissance Art I
20	Explorers	Caribbean Sea	Motors	Renaissance Art II

www.Layers-of-Learning.com

3	History	Geography	Science	The Arts
1	Age of Exploration	Argentina & Chile	Classification & Insects	Fairy Tales
2	The Ottoman Empire	Egypt & Libya	Reptiles & Amphibians	Poetry
3	Mogul Empire	Pakistan & Afghanistan	Fish	Mogul Arts
4	Reformation	Angola & Zambia	Birds	Reformation Art
5	Renaissance England	Tanzania & Kenya	Mammals & Primates	Shakespeare
6	Thirty Years' War	Spain	Sound	Baroque Music
7	The Dutch	Netherlands	Light & Optics	Baroque Art I
8	France	Indonesia	Bending Light	Baroque Art II
9	The Enlightenment	Korean Peninsula	Color	Art Journaling
10	Russia & Prussia	Central Asia	History of Science	Watercolors
11	Conquistadors	Baltic States	Igneous Rocks	Creative Kids
12	Settlers	Peru & Bolivia	Sedimentary Rocks	Native American Art
13	13 Colonies	Central America	Metamorphic Rocks	Settler Sayings
14	Slave Trade	Brazil	Gems & Minerals	Colonial Art
15	The South Pacific	Australasia	Fossils	Principles of Art
16	The British in India	India	Chemical Reactions	Classical Music
17	The Boston Tea Party	Japan	Reversible Reactions	Folk Music
18	Founding Fathers	Iran	Compounds & Solutions	Rococo
19	Declaring Independence	Samoa & Tonga	Oxidation & Reduction	Creative Crafts I
20	The American Revolution	South Africa	Acids & Bases	Creative Crafts II

4	History	Geography	Science	The Arts
1	American Government	USA	Heat & Temperature	Patriotic Music
2	Expanding Nation	Pacific States	Motors & Engines	Tall Tales
3	Industrial Revolution	U.S. Landscapes	Energy	Romantic Art I
4	Revolutions	Mountain West States	Energy Sources	Romantic Art II
5	Africa	U.S. Political Maps	Energy Conversion	Impressionism I
6	The West	Southwest States	Earth Structure	Impressionism II
7	Civil War	National Parks	Plate Tectonics	Post Impressionism
8	World War I	Plains States	Earthquakes	Expressionism
9	Totalitarianism	U.S. Economics	Volcanoes	Abstract Art
10	Great Depression	Heartland States	Mountain Building	Kinds of Art
11	World War II	Symbols & Landmarks	Chemistry of Air & Water	War Art
12	Modern East Asia	The South	Food Chemistry	Modern Art
13	India's Independence	People of America	Industry	Pop Art
14	Israel	Appalachian States	Chemistry of Farming	Modern Music
15	Cold War	U.S. Territories	Chemistry of Medicine	Free Verse
16	Vietnam War	Atlantic States	Food Chains	Photography
17	Latin America	New England States	Animal Groups	Latin American Art
18	Civil Rights	Home State Study I	Instincts	Theater & Film
19	Technology	Home State Study II	Habitats	Architecture
20	Terrorism	America in Review	Conservation	Creative Kids

Unit 4-6 Printable Pack

This unit includes printables at the end. To make life easier for you we also created digital printable packs for each unit. To retrieve your printable pack for Unit 4-6, please visit

www.layers-of-learning.com/digital-printable-packs/

Put the printable pack in your shopping cart and use this coupon code:

3131UNIT4-6

Your printable pack will be free.

Layers of Learning Introduction

This is part of a series of units in the Layers of Learning homeschool curriculum, including the subjects of history, geography, science, and the arts. Children from 1st through 12th can participate in the same curriculum at the same time - family school style.

The units are intended to be used in order as the basis of a complete curriculum (once you add in a systematic math, reading, and writing program). You begin with Year 1 Unit 1 no matter what ages your children are. Spend about 2 weeks on each unit. You pick and choose the activities within the unit that appeal to you and read the books from the book list that are available to you or find others on the same topic from your library. We highly recommend that you use the timeline in every history section as the backbone. Then flesh out your learning with reading and activities that highlight the topics you think are the most important.

Alternatively, you can use the units as activity ideas to supplement another curriculum in any order you wish. You can still use them with all ages of children at the same time.

When you've finished with Year One, move on to Year Two, Year Three, and Year Four. Then begin again with Year One and work your way through the years again. Now your children will be older, reading more involved books, and writing more in depth. When you have completed the sequence for the second time, you start again on it for the third and final time. If your student began with Layers of Learning in 1st grade and stayed with it all the way through she would go through the four year rotation three times, firmly cementing the information in her mind in ever increasing depth. At each level you should expect increasing amounts of outside reading and writing. High schoolers in particular should be reading extensively, and if possible, participating in discussion groups.

These icons will guide you in spotting activities and books that are appropriate for the age of child you are working with. But if you think an activity is too juvenile or too difficult for your kids, adjust accordingly. The icons are not there as rules, just guides.

☺ 1st-4th

☻ 5th-8th

☻ 9th-12th

Within each unit we share:

EXPLORATIONS, activities relating to the topic;
EXPERIMENTS, usually associated with science topics;
EXPEDITIONS, field trips;
EXPLANATIONS, teacher helps or educational philosophies.

In the sidebars we also include Additional Layers, Famous Folks, Fabulous Facts, On the Web, and other extra related topics that can take you off on tangents, exploring the world and your interests with a bit more freedom. The curriculum will always be there to pull you back on track when you're ready.

www.layers-of-learning.com

UNIT SIX
THE WEST - SOUTHWEST STATES - EARTH STRUCTURE - IMPRESSIONISM II

I went to the woods because I wished to live deliberately, to front only the essential facts of life, and see if I could not learn what it had to teach, and not, when I came to die, discover that I had not lived.
-Henry David Thoreau

LIBRARY LIST

HISTORY

Search for: westward expansion, pioneers, mountain men, Pony Express, Oregon Trail, gold rush, Indian Wars, Mexican-American War

☺ Wagon Wheels by Barbara Brenner. The story of a family of three motherless boys and their father as they head west to make new lives.

☺ The California Gold Rush by Mel Friedman.

☺ ☻ Little House on the Prairie Series by Laura Ingalls Wilder. A great read aloud.

☺ ☻ Westward Expansion by Teresa Domnauer.

☺ ☻ Caddie Woodlawn by Carol Ryrie Brink. Fictional pioneer story based on the author's grandmother.

☻ The Tragic Tale of Narcissa Whitman and a Faithful History of the Oregon Trail by Cheryl Harness.

☻ The Oregon Trail: An Interactive History Adventure by Matt Doeden.

☻ The California Gold Rush: An Interactive History Adventure by Elizabeth Raum.

☻ A Pioneer Sampler: The Daily Life of a Pioneer Family in 1840 by Barbara Greenwood.

☻ The Split History of Westward Expansion by Nell Musolf. Read the book front to back about the pioneer experience, then flip the book over and read it the other way for the Native American experience.

☻ Moccasin Trail by Eloise Jarvis McGraw. A young boy runs away to the west, is nearly killed, but is saved by Crow Indians. What happens when he meets his younger siblings traveling west by themselves?

☻ Daily Life in a Plains Indian Village 1868 by Michael Terry.

☻ By the Great Horn Spoon! by Sid Fleishman. A young boy and his manservant set out to the gold fields of California to save their family from poverty.

☻ ☻ The Mexican-American War by John DiConsiglio.

☻ Lions of the West: Heroes and Villains of the Westward Expansion by Robert Morgan.

☻ Civil Disobedience by Henry David Thoreau.

☻ The Apache Wars by Paul Andrew Hutton. A longish book, full of details, violence, cheating, lying, and destruction on both sides.

☻ My Sixty Years on the Plains: Trapping, Trading, and Indian Fighting by W.T. Hamilton. This is a memoir from a real life mountain man.

☻ Indian Wars by Robert M. Utley and Wilcomb E. Washburn.

GEOGRAPHY	Search for: New Mexico, Arizona, Texas, Oklahoma, American Southwest, U.S. States ☺ G is For Grand Canyon: An Arizona Alphabet by Barbara Gowan. ☺ L is for Lonestar: A Texas Alphabet by Alan Stacy. ☺ E is For Enchantment: A New Mexico Alphabet by Helen Foster James. ☺ This is Texas by Miroslav Sasek. ☻ Children of the Dustbowl: The True Story of the School at Weedpatch Camp by Jerry Stanley. A really interesting true story about the impact of the Dust Bowl in the southwest. ☻ Arizona by Dan Filbin. ☻ Forgotten Tales of New Mexico by Ellen Dornan.
SCIENCE	Search for: structure of the earth, layers of the earth, earth science ☺ The Magic School Bus Inside the Earth by Joanna Cole. ☺ Planet Earth/Inside Out by Gail Gibbons. ☺ ☻ Earth's Layers: Our Changing Earth by Jason D. Nemeth. ☻ Smithsonian: Earth by Douglas Palmer, et al. Use this book as a basic text for Units 4-6 through 4-10.
THE ARTS	Search for: Impressionism, Claude Monet, Auguste Renoir, Alfred Sisley, Frederic Bazille, Camille Pisarro, Edouard Manet, Paul Cezanne, Berthe Morisot, Edgar Degas, Mary Cassatt, American Impressionism. ☺ Linnea in Monet's Garden by Christina Bjork and Lena Anderson. This is a beautiful picture book about Linnea, a little girl who visits Monet's Japanese foot bridge and learns about Impressionist art. ☺ Monet Paints A Day by Julie Danneberg. A picture book that not only tells a story, but also has notes and letters from Monet. ☺ What Degas Saw by Samantha Friedman. A picture book about Degas walking through Paris with the eyes of an artist. ☺ Degas and the Little Dancer by Laurence Anholt. ☺ ☻ Pierre Auguste Renoir by Mike Venezia. This is from the *Getting To Know The World's Greatest Artists* series. Look for other Impressionist artists in this series by the same author. ☺ ☻ Who Was Claude Monet? by Ann Waldron. ☺ ☻ Impressionism: 13 Artists Children Should Know by Florian Heine. ☺ ☻ ☻ Eyewitness: Manet by Patricia Wright. Look for other artists in this series as well. Lots of pictures and tidbits of information. ☺ ☻ ☻ Impressionists from Monet to Van Gogh: Coloring Book by Florence Gentner and Dominique Foufelle. This isn't just a coloring book, it's a color by numbers that intends to help you create Impressionist masterpieces. Dover Publishing also sells inexpensive versions of Impressionist coloring books. ☺ ☻ Eyewitness: Impressionism by Jude Welton.

HISTORY: THE WEST

Additional Layer

Many Americans at the time of the Mexican-American War believed the war was unjust. Henry David Thoreau was one of these. He refused to pay his taxes because he was unwilling to support the war in any form.

Thoreau was put in jail because of his tax protest, but bailed out a few days later by a female relative who was embarrassed by his behavior. He wrote the book *Civil Disobedience* to explain his method of protesting the government. His book greatly influenced Martin Luther King Jr. and Mahatma Gandhi. You should read it.

As you learn more about the Mexican-American War decide for yourself if you think it was unjust.

During the 1800s America expanded rapidly, stretching ultimately from sea to sea. The Louisiana Purchase of 1803 nearly doubled the size of the United States. It didn't take long at all for Americans to begin to move into the new territories. By the 1820s the Mississippi River was already the frontier of the new country.

Most the rest of the west was claimed by Mexico, although, aside from coastal cities in California, there were no Mexican settlers in the region. In 1848 the new Mexican government, recently liberated from Spain, attacked a garrison of U.S. Army soldiers who were pursuing bandits in Mexican territory. The United States declared war and marched their army and marines clear into Mexico City. The Mexicans sued for peace and were given back all of their southern territories. The United States retained the land in the north, stretching from Texas to California.

Farmers poured into the fertile lands of the Willamette Valley in Oregon Territory as well. This land was still claimed by Britain, but the United States government encouraged settlement in Oregon. They wanted to flood the territory with Americans who could then be used as a basis to claim the land for America. It worked, and a treaty was signed with Britain in 1846, making the 49th parallel the permanent boundary between the United States and Canada.

The new American territory included the land in Utah, recently settled by the Mormons who had been fleeing persecution in Missouri and then Illinois. There were also mountain men and Christian missionaries scattered across the land. And of course, there were still many Native American tribes living in the newly claimed America.

In 1848, just after the war with Mexico was concluded, gold was discovered at Sutter's Mill, California. From this point Americans and immigrants poured into California, Nevada, and Colorado searching for gold. The transcontinental railroad was finished in 1869 and the west was finally and irrevocably open to civilization.

☺ ☺ ☺ **EXPLORATION: Timeline**
At the end of this unit you will find printable timeline cards to cut apart and place on a timeline on a wall or in a notebook.

- May 1846 Mexican forces ambush two American companies and President Polk declares war on Mexico

- 1846 Mormon pioneers begin their westward migration
- 1846-1869 Peak years of the Oregon Trail
- January 1848 Gold is discovered in California
- February 1848 Treaty of Guadalupe Hidalgo is signed, ceding land of Texas, New Mexico, and California to the U.S. from Mexico
- September 1850 California is admitted as a free state
- 1851 Indian Appropriations Act expands reservation system to the west
- 1854 13,000 Chinese immigrants enter the U.S. in California to work in gold mines and on the railroad
- 1860-61 Pony Express mail service
- 1862 Homestead Act gives 160 acres of free western land to anyone who would agree to live on and work the land.
- 1862 Dakota War in Minnesota
- 1863 Gold discovered in Montana
- 1864 Sand Creek Massacre, Colorado, triggers the Plains Wars
- 1866 Mining companies granted titles to millions of acres of western lands
- May 1869 First transcontinental railroad is completed at Promontory Point, Utah
- 1874 Gold discovered in the sacred lands of the Lakota, the Black Hills; instigates another Sioux war
- June 1876 Battle of Little Bighorn
- 1877 Nez Perce War led by Chief Joseph
- 1878 Cheyenne escape from Oklahoma reservation; pursued by the army all the way to Montana homelands; hundreds die
- 1882 Chinese Exclusion Act banned Chinese immigration
- 1885 Geronimo leads a band of Apache off the reservation
- February 1887 Dawes Act, intended to integrate Indians into American society, actually creates federal dependence and takes away some of the reservation land previously given
- 1889 Indian Territory (Oklahoma) is opened to the public as free land. Settlers race across the territory claiming all 1.92 million acres by sunset on the first day
- December 1890 U.S. Army troops massacre 300 Indians at Wounded Knee, including women and children; marks the end of significant Native American resistance
- 1893 An estimated 2,000 buffalo remain of the original 20 million that once roamed the western plains
- February 1912 Arizona is the last of the contiguous 48 states to be admitted to the Union.

☺ ☺ ☺ **EXPLORATION: Map of Expanding Nation**
This map activity shows how the nation was expanding and when

Additional Layer

In 1882 President Chester A. Arthur signed into law the "Chinese Exclusion Act" which cut off nearly all Chinese immigration to the United States.

Many at the time decried the act as legalized racial discrimination, but it remained the law until 1943. Learn more about the law, why it was passed, and the consequences for Americans and for ethnic Chinese.

Immigration has been a hot topic in the United States since the Naturalization Act of 1790 barred naturalization of non-whites.

What principles do you think the immigration laws should be based on? Are there any who should be excluded? Should immigration be completely open and free or should numbers be restricted? Why? Think about the pros and cons.

Additional Layer

The territories of the United States were gained through either treaty and purchase or through armed conflict.

The Pig War was a bloodless conflict "fought" for over a decade between the United States and Britain over the ownership of the San Juan Islands which lie between Victoria Island and the mainland of Washington State. Read more about it to learn how pigs and potatoes nearly caused an international incident.

https://www.nps.gov/sajh/learn/historycul-ture/the-pig-war.htm

On the Web

This site has photos, direct quotes, and explanations about the life of a mountain man. http://xroads.virginia.edu/~hy-per/hns/mtmen/home.html

Famous Folks

James Beckwourth was a former slave turned mountain man. He narrated a book about his experiences, *The Life and Adventures of James P. Beckwourth: Mountaineer, Scout and Pioneer, and Chief of the Crow Nation of Indians.*

each of the territories was added. It includes wagon trails, the Pony Express route, important settlements, and landmarks.

Color the rivers and other water first, then the wagon trail routes, Pony Express symbols, and fort symbols. Then carefully outline each of the territory additions. There are lots of lines on the map, so kids may need some help. Use the colored map below as a reference.

While your kids work, read aloud or talk about westward expansion, landmarks, and routes.

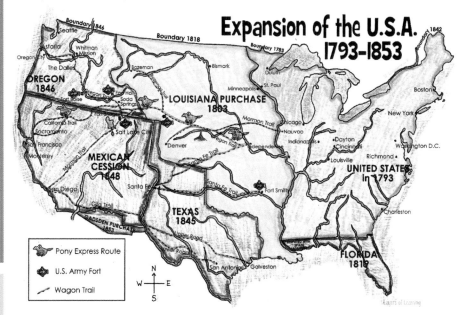

☺ ☺ EXPLORATION: Mountain Men

Mountain men were trappers and hunters who went off into the western American and Canadian wilderness alone or in small groups hunting beaver. Most mountain men traveled the Rocky Mountains in the years between 1810 and 1880. Some were self-employed, but most worked for large fur trading companies. After the fur trade began to die out, they were often hired by wagon trains to guide the settlers west or by the army as scouts. In fact, it was the mountain men and the fur trading companies that explored, mapped, and created the trails that later settlers followed west.

Every year the mountain men and the fur buyers would meet up at a rendezvous in the spring or summer. The mountain men would bring their furs to sell and the trading companies would bring in mule trains of whiskey, tools, supplies, and food to sell to the trappers. Indians, mountain men, wives, and children would all gather for weeks of music, dancing, gaming, and contests. Many

mountain men spent their whole year's fur take at the rendezvous.

Mountain men carried their few possessions with them wherever they went. They generally had mules or horses, one for riding and one as a pack animal to carry their supplies. They carried cooking pots, utensils, axes, guns, knives, powder, lead shot, traps, pemmican, tobacco, coffee, and salt, plus whatever furs they had gathered. The things they needed to get their hands on quickly, like shot and powder or a supply of tobacco, were kept in a pouch slung around their bodies and across one shoulder.

Make your own possibles pouch. You will need fabric, scissors, a needle, and thread. This can be hand sewn or you can sew it on a sewing machine. Using wool or felt will mean you don't have to do any hemming. We used an old wool army blanket.

1. Start by cutting a long rectangle. You can see the dimensions of our bag and strap below. This one is fairly large and was made for a teenager. You can scale it down for younger kids.

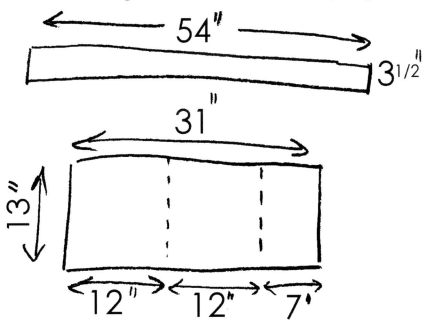

2. The dotted lines on the pattern above show where the bag was folded to make the pouch and the lid. Fold along the right hand line and sew up the two sides. The next photo shows you how the two side seams look when they are inside out.

Famous Folks

John Colter was a member of the Lewis and Clark Expedition and later explored the west as a mountain man and fur trapper, but he is most famous for "Colter's Run."

Captured by hostile Indians, his companion was killed, but Colter was stripped naked and told to run. He ran, and the braves pursued him. The only one who could keep up was killed by Colter, who then hid underwater in a log jam until the rest gave up the search. Colter then walked 200 miles to the nearest fort, naked, except for a blanket he had stolen from the brave he killed.

Famous Folks

The only thing tougher than surviving the winter in the Rocky Mountains alone is doing it with two small children.

Marie Dorion crossed the Rockies several times with her two small children, both with trading companies and alone, fighting for survival. She used her horses' tail hairs to craft snares to trap animals to eat, foraged for the bark of trees, and evaded enemy Indians.

Expedition

Interstate 80 runs from San Francisco, California to Teaneck, New Jersey. It follows the route of the old westward trails of expansion including the Lincoln Highway (the first road across America), a portion of the Oregon Trail (through Nebraska and Wyoming), the Mormon Trail (to Salt Lake City), the California Trail, and the Pony Express Route. The Mormon and California Trails branched off of the Oregon Trail in Wyoming.

Travel along a portion of this road with your family, noticing the landscape and imagining what it would have been like to be a pioneer traveling the road in a wagon. Where would you camp?

If you'll be in Wyoming check out these sites: http://www.tourwyoming.com/things-to-do/activities/trails/

This series of guides from the National Park Service will help as well: https://www.nps.gov/oreg/plan-yourvisit/index.htm

Here are guides specific to the Pony Express Routes: https://www.nps.gov/poex/index.htm

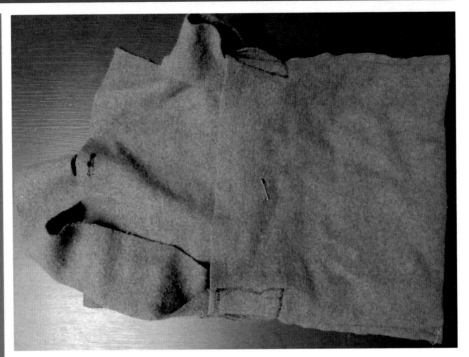

3. Then sew the strap on. We used a zig-zag stitch on a sewing machine to make ours really strong. If you are sewing by hand, double your thread for extra strength and sew around the strap twice to make the stitching more durable. In the photo below you can see how the strap is attached.

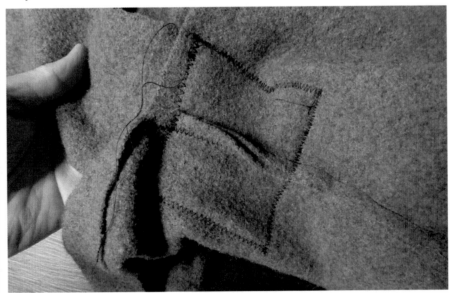

4. You can sew a button to hold the flap closed if you like.

☺ ☻ EXPLORATION: Westward Migration

From approximately 1836 until the railroads were completed in the late 1800s, pioneers were traveling west in search of land and opportunity.

While traveling, they were exposed to every kind of weather. The farm and frontier families worked outside most of the time even after they reached their destinations. They needed protection from the elements, especially from the heat of the sun. Even in hot weather they wore long sleeves

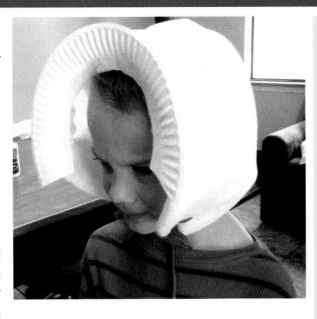

and long pants and hats with wide brims to keep the sun off.

Make a pioneer bonnet. You need a rectangle of muslin fabric in either calico or a plain color.

1. Cut your fabric into a rectangle. Mine was about 23 inches by 12 inches to fit a six year old. Make it bigger for bigger kids.
2. Cut out a rim from a paper plate, keeping just over half of the rim.
3. Glue the long side of the fabric to the paper plate rim, gathering as you go.

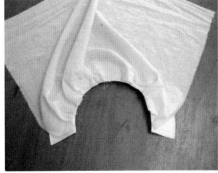

4. Let the glue dry, then cut small slits across the opposite side of the fabric and thread the ribbon through the slit.

☺ EXPLORATION: Oxen

Pioneers almost always used oxen to pull their wagons. Horses

Additional Layer

Imagine putting your family's possessions, food, and tools in a wagon or handcart and setting off into the wilderness. What would you need most? Make a supply list.

Photo by Verne Equinox, CC license, Wikimedia

Fabulous Facts

The trip west was challenging for all pioneers, but for some companies it was deadly. The Donner Party decided to take a "shortcut," ended up lost and delayed for months, and got caught in the heavy snows of the Sierra Nevada Mountains, where most of them perished and the rest were driven to cannibalism.

The Martin and Willie handcart companies left too late in the season and were caught in early snows in Wyoming where about half of them died before rescue.

Read more.

were expensive and not nearly as strong as an ox. Oxen could also eat almost any green thing and go without water for longer than a horse. Oxen also didn't get sick as much as horses. Once the pioneers made it out west they needed the strength of the oxen to pull out stumps and plow the virgin fields.

Make an oxen mask.

1. Use the printable at the end of this unit. Print it on brown paper or have your kids color it in.
2. Cut apart the horns, ears, and face. Glue everything together in the right order.
3. Add wiggly eyes attached way to the left and right. Oxen have eyes on the sides of their heads.
4. Add a fringe of woolly hair on the forehead by cutting a strip of brown paper into a rectangle, then cutting slits to make a fringe. Curl the paper around a pencil to make it curly. Glue it in place.
5. Make the face into a mask by cutting eye holes and adding a paper strip to keep it secured to the head.

Get out a wagon and let your kids play pioneer, taking turns being the oxen and the pioneer riding.

☺ ☺ ☺ EXPLORATION: Oregon Country

Oregon Country included most of British Columbia; all of Washington, Idaho, and Oregon; and parts of Montana and Wyoming. The region was explored and mapped by British and French trappers in the early 1800s and by Lewis and Clark in 1803, but the Spanish had explored the coastline even earlier in the late 1700s. Spain, France, Russia, the United States, and Britain all claimed the land at one point. Spain, Russia, and France all gave up their claims through treaty, leaving only Britain and the United States with claims.

This is a map of Oregon Country by Kmusser, CC license, Wikimedia

The British were the first to establish settlements in the region through the Hudson's Bay Company. By the 1830s American settlers with families were moving in and beginning to farm, and American missionaries were setting up missions and teaching the natives to read and write and know Jesus. By the 1840s the trickle of American immigrants became a flood. In 1846 the British negotiated a treaty to settle the border between British Canada and the Oregon Territory of the United States at the 49th parallel.

The Willamette Valley, located in Oregon, is filled with extremely fertile soil that was deposited thousands of years ago during the Missoula flood and the last Ice Age. It is surrounded on three sides by mountain ranges: the Cascades, the Oregon Coast Range and the Calapooya Mountains. It is sheltered and well-watered both with rainfall and by rivers from the mountains. The weather is warm, only occasionally hot, and mild with few storms. This became the destination of most of the early settlers to the region.

Visit this site to learn more about the pioneers of Oregon Country: http://www.oregonpioneers.com/ortrail.htm, and watch this short film about Oregon Country on YouTube: "Oregon Trail Learn About Pioneer Life".

After you have learned more about Oregon pioneers, make some pioneer paper dolls and create a script of a day-in-the-life of an Oregon Pioneer. Act out your story with your paper dolls.

☺ ☻ **EXPLORATION: The Story of the Mormons**
The Mormon church, officially The Church of Jesus Christ of Latter-day Saints, was begun in 1836 in New York State by Joseph Smith. At this time many religious sects were begun, most fizzling out quickly. But the Mormon faith grew. They grouped together in communities and, because of persecution, moved from place to place, from New York to Kirkland, Ohio, then Jackson County, Missouri.

In Missouri the church got caught up in the debate over slavery. Church members were anti-slavery northerners for the most part and voted against pro-slavery measures. Democrats at this point were very keen on spreading slavery, and since each territory got to decide whether it would be slave or free, they hounded and persecuted everyone whose politics were the wrong brand.

Besides the political aspect, Mormons were an easy target because they were different. They tended to keep to themselves, not mixing with the community; they had odd religious views; and they kept pouring in, disrupting the established order. In Missouri Mormon property was destroyed. Mormon men were

Fabulous Fact
The first government of Oregon Country was the Provisional Government of Oregon. At first they wanted to become their own nation, but by 1848 the political pressure to join the United States was fierce, and so the Oregonians gave in without a fight.

Learning about this provisional government can give you some insight into how people first form governments from nothing, though these people did have the knowledge and history of Europe and the United States to base their ideas on.

Additional Layer
Upstate New York, in the area where Joseph Smith lived as a boy, was known as the "burned over district" because the people were all "burning" with the Spirit, or religious zeal. Priests and preachers of established sects like the Episcopalians and Baptists held revival meetings that were attended by hundreds. Many new sects, all claiming to have the truth, sprung up in this environment as well.

This is called the Second Great Awakening.

Famous Folks

Brigham Young was the leader of the Mormons who led them to the Utah valleys to settle. Besides being the head of the church, he also became the territorial governor.

Additional Layer

In 1857 President James Buchanan sent U.S. Army forces to the Salt Lake Valley to put an end to polygamy, the Mormon practice of marrying more than one wife, and to ascertain the theocracy which had been created by Brigham Young. The Mormons were alarmed and set about to disrupt the army as much as possible without resorting to armed conflict.

During this crisis Mormon men fell upon and massacred a California wagon train, killing 120 innocent and unarmed men, women, and children, leaving no witnesses in the Mountain Meadows Massacre.

tarred and feathered. Mormon women were raped. And Mormons were killed. The massacre at Haun's Mill was the worst tragedy of these days. It followed an extermination order given by the governor of the state, Lilburn Boggs. Executive Order #44 said that Mormons were to be exterminated or driven from the state. Joseph Smith was imprisoned in Liberty, Missouri. The rest of the Mormons fled. Many of them left on foot in winter with no preparation or provisions.

They walked to Illinois where they found help from the local settlers and later founded a new city which they named Nauvoo. For a decade there was peace, but the Mormons quickly dominated politics, economics, and social life in Illinois. Nauvoo was the largest city. This, along with practices such as polygamy, created tension with neighbors, and the persecutions started up again. In 1844 Joseph Smith was arrested and, while in jail in Carthage, Illinois, he and his brother, Hyrum, were murdered by a mob.

Within a year, the charter of the city of Nauvoo had been revoked, and Mormons in outlying settlements had been driven from their homes again. They decided to head west into the wilderness.

The first wagon trains left in 1846, wintered on the plains, and reached the Salt Lake Valley, which was far from other settlers. It was part of Mexico when they arrived in 1847. Over the next twenty years 70,000 people traveled the Mormon Trail to the Salt Lake Valley.

Many Mormon families were too poor to afford the wagons and teams and supplies that would allow them to travel west. Instead of costly wagons and teams, they built much smaller handcarts which could be pushed or pulled by people, usually a man and his wife and children. They couldn't bring much with them, mostly just the food they would need on the trip and some blankets, tools, and cooking supplies.

This site has many different pioneer journals (some Mormon, some California, and some Oregon) scanned so that you can see the original journal and the handwriting on each page. The pages have also been transcribed to make them much easier to read. http://overlandtrails.lib.byu.edu/

Write your own pioneer journal as though you were traveling along the trail headed west. Before you write, decide why you are traveling west, where you are headed, and who you are with. Write as though you are somewhere on the trail. Include an interesting event. Date the entry for sometime in the 1850s.

☺ ☻ EXPLORATION: Plains Indians

Some of the tribes of the Great Plains of the United States and Canada were nomadic hunter-gatherers. They developed a horse culture, became expert riders, and hunted game such as deer, elk, and buffalo from the backs of their horses. They used spears, bows, and clubs. They also learned to make war on horseback. Because they moved so often with the herds, they did not live in permanent villages. Instead they built teepees, movable homes that they could dismantle and carry with them.

You can watch this YouTube video "Lakota- Native Americans of the Great Plains" to learn more about the Plains Indians.

After you have read and learned more, make a teepee craft. You will need a paper plate, scissors, crayons or markers, sticks, and glue.
1. Fold the paper plate in half and cut along the fold.
2. Decorate the half circle in the style of the Plains Indians.
3. Cut a slit in the center along the curved edge to make an entry

Additional Layer

American cowboys were ranch workers who tended cattle. After the Civil War the demand for beef in the United States skyrocketed, and cattle ranching on the Great Plains and in Texas became profitable. Cattle were allowed to roam feral on the open range and then were rounded up in the spring. The calves were branded to show ownership and the older ones were herded north to the meat packing plants in Chicago. Today cowboys still ride the range looking after their herds.

Learn more about the cowboy lifestyle.

Famous Folks

Kit Carson was a mountain man, army scout, and wilderness guide. He ran away at age 16 to live in the mountains and fight Indians. In later life his attitudes toward the Indians softened, and he became a fair and compassionate Indian agent for the U.S. government.

On The Web

Read this first hand account by Hugh McGinnis, a member of the 7th Cavalry Division that attacked the Indians at the Wounded Knee Massacre. http://www.ourfamilyhistory.biz/woundedknee.htm

Fabulous Fact

The Grattan Massacre started the Sioux Wars. Soldiers went to a Sioux camp to arrest a cow thief. The Indians refused, the soldiers killed the chief, and the Sioux killed 31 soldiers.

Writer's Workshop

Write about whether or not you agree with this quote by Ralph Peters:

"The nature of warfare never changes, only its superficial manifestations. Joshua and David, Hector and Achilles would recognize the combat that our soldiers and Marines have waged in the alleys of Somalia and Iraq. The uniforms evolve, bronze gives way to titanium, arrows may be replaced by laser-guided bombs, but the heart of the matter is still killing your enemies until any survivors surrender and do your will."

flap.

4. Curve the circle around to make a cone. Glue some short sticks at the top of the cone so they will stick out as though they are tent poles. We used hot glue.
5. Glue the two sides of the tent together in a cone.

☺ ☻ EXPLORATION: Plains Indians Wars

Early immigrants to the land west of the Mississippi made treaties with the Indian tribes. Relations between Native Americans and settlers were mostly peaceful. But gold rushes in Colorado, Montana, and the Black Hills brought more settlers into direct competition with the natives. Soon land rushes followed. The United States government felt pressure to provide more land to clamoring settlers; treaties with the tribes were broken.

In 1865, with the Civil War over, the new policy of the United States was to force Indians onto reservations where they would be assimilated into American culture. The Army set up outposts and forts in the wilderness to subdue the natives and protect the settlers. Bands on the warpath were hunted down and defeated. Villages of women and children were rounded up and put on reservations. In a couple of instances unarmed Indians, including men, women, and children of all ages, were mowed down by the guns of soldiers or renegade civilians.

Many tribes fought back, desperate to retain their lands and way of life. But it was the Sioux of the northern plains and the Apache of the Southwest who mounted the stiffest resistance.

Red Cloud of the Lakota Sioux attacked and defeated Captain William J. Fetterman and his troop of 81 men. Fetterman was pursuing a small band that had attacked some wood cutters on the previous day. Ahead of him Fetterman saw a group of a few Indians led by a man on a lame horse. The small group led Fetterman right into an ambush. The man on the lame horse was Red Cloud himself, the fearless chief, who had planned the whole attack. Every man of Fetterman's party was killed while only 14 Lakota lost their lives. This massacre caused the United States government to back down and sign the treaty of Fort Laramie in 1868. The treaty gave the Sioux exclusive ownership of the Black Hills and hunting rights over vast swaths of land in Montana, Wyoming, and South Dakota. After gold was discovered in the Black Hills, the U.S. government seized the land, and war broke out once more. The Sioux were subdued. In 1980 the Lakota Sioux sued the U.S. government for the Black Hills and won a huge monetary settlement, but the tribe refused the money, saying they wanted the land back instead.

Plains Indians wore war bonnets when they went into battle, at ceremonies, and during important political talks within the tribe or between tribes. The feathers in the bonnet were earned by doing great acts of selfless valor. To earn an eagle feather was the highest possible honor in the tribe. Other feathers from golden eagles, owls, and so forth would also be awarded for various deeds.

Make an Indian style headdress from construction paper.

1. Start with a sheet of 12" x 18" brown or yellow construction paper. Fold it in half the long way. Cut it along the fold.
2. Fold each side in half the long way again. Cut along that fold as well.
3. Tape or glue three of the strips to one another along the short sides to make one long strip. Decorate the strip with traditional Native American patterns.
4. Use the fourth strip to make a headband that fits around your child's head in the center of the longer strip. You will end up with a headband with two long strips hanging down from the back.
5. Now cut feathers out of construction paper; make them 12 inches long. Glue them along the headdress from the center all of the way down the long strips. If you would like, you can give one feather at a time to your child to add to his or her headdress as he or she does things that are generous, brave, kind, or above the average.

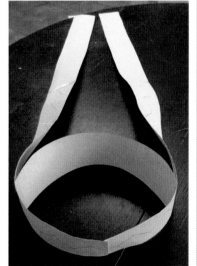

Fabulous Fact

The wild west was tamed in part by the railroads. There had been a race to complete the lines connecting east and west. In 1869 the final ceremonial golden spike was driven at Promontory, Utah.

Famous Folks

General George Custer is best known for dying spectacularly in a Lakota attack that became known as Custer's Last Stand. Before that he was a celebrated Civil War officer and participated in Reconstruction.

Additional Layer

The Plains Indians Wars are an example of asymmetrical conflict, which means that one side had a large advantage over the other. In the case of the United States versus the Indians, the advantage lay in both numbers and technology.

Other categories of war include total war, biological war, chemical war, conventional war, unconventional war, cyber war, nuclear war, war of aggression, defensive war, and civil war.

Which of these do you think would apply to the Plains Wars? Why?

Additional Layer

Apache families voluntarily settled near Camp Grant in Arizona, where the military commanders had been kind, giving out rations and helping the natives to find work selling hay to the army and harvesting crops for local ranchers.

Many locals were upset though, believing the Camp Grant Apaches to be responsible for every depredation in the area.

A force of civilians (Mexican, American, and rival O'odham tribesmen) attacked the Camp Grant people when the men were away in the mountains. 136 women and children and 8 men were killed and scalped.

Despite the threat of martial law from the United States government and protests, only a mock trial was ever held. And the perpetrators unfairly got off scot-free.

Fabulous Fact

Clipper Ships were fast trading vessels that traveled the world oceans in the 1800s. They were important in the California Gold Rush as they carried people and supplies from New York to San Francisco.

☺ ☺ ☺ EXPLORATION: Apache Wars

The wars with the Apache began in the same way other Indian wars began. Settlers (in this case gold prospectors in the Santa Rita mountains) moved into territory that belonged to the Apaches by treaty. The Apache attacked to defend their territory, and Americans retaliated. At first the attacks were perpetuated by groups of miners or settlers. Later the military got involved. The incidents escalated with the Apaches attacking, torturing, kidnapping, and murdering civilian and military targets and the Americans doing likewise. There were atrocities on both sides.

In 1864 the government decided to force the Apache, Navajo, and other tribes onto reservations. First they burned and destroyed their crops and homes and then sent the army to escort them to Bosque Redondo Reservation. This forced march is known as the Long Walk. The reservation was a disaster. Rival tribes were placed in the same area, and conflicts arose. There wasn't enough clean water or firewood. The crops failed repeatedly because of man-made and natural disasters. After a few years the Navajo initiated their own Long Walk and returned home. The government let them go. While the experience was devastating for the Navajo, it also forged them into one strong, tight knit nation where before they had been rival tribes.

The Apache continued to resist and mount raiding and war parties for decades. Geronimo was the most famous of the war band leaders. When the U.S. government tried to move the Apaches onto the San Carlos Reservation in 1876, about half of the Apache tribe fled to Mexico under Geronimo's leadership. Geronimo and his men continued their attacks but were eventually captured and led to the reservation. Geronimo surrendered and escaped three times. The Apache way of life was nomadic and relied on raiding enemies for gain, and so the reservation life, dependent on government handouts and restricted in movement, was unbearable for many Apache. Whenever they were off of the reservation the Apache spent their time raiding wagon trains, ranches, and small villages in both Mexico and the United States. Usually during these raids they would kill everyone so as not to leave behind any witnesses.

The U.S. government was anxious to bring an end to these attacks. They received permission from Mexico to pursue the Apache across the border and recruited Apache scouts to guide them to the renegade bands. Eventually Geronimo was captured and sent to Florida and then Oklahoma as a prisoner of war. The U.S. Army moved quickly to relocate him so that Geronimo would not be tried by the civil authorities for murder, for which he surely would have been hanged. Later in life he became a celebrity as crowds would line the streets to see him riding in parades or throng to fairs to see him dressed in his traditional Apache garb. Apache raids and attacks continued until 1924.

Read about Apache culture on this site: http://americanindian-originals.com/apache-indian.html and on this one: http://www.wmat.nsn.us/history.html. Then make a diorama or poster showing the Apache way of life. Add some written captions and short descriptions to your project.

☺ ☺ ☻ EXPLORATION: Miner '49er

In 1848 California was annexed by the United States following the Mexican-American War and a brief stint as the independent Bear Republic. The economy was based on cattle, agriculture, timber, and the supplying of ships in the Pacific. Then gold was discovered at Sutter's Mill, and California changed over night.

In 1849, and for years afterward, gold prospectors, mostly from the eastern United States (but also from Asia, Australia, Europe, and Latin America), poured into California to try their luck. San Francisco exploded from a village of 1,000 in 1848 to a booming city of 25,000 just two years later. These prospectors became known as '49ers because they traveled to California with the gold rush of 1849.

Very few made it rich, but they all impacted the state in some way. By far the largest population was men. Government resources and laws were scarce, property rights were not established, foreigners (non white Americans) were systematically discriminated against, forced out, and sometimes even hunted, and there was a great deal of liquor. California became violent.

This YouTube video is an excellent introduction to the Gold Rush of 1849: "The Start of the California Gold Rush".

You can pan for gold like a miner '49er. First, get dressed in miner clothes: blue jeans and a button down shirt. Add boots and a wide brimmed hat if you have them.

Next, you'll need some gold nuggets and a river bed. You can spray paint some pebbles gold or use yellow or gold colored beads. For the river use a kiddie pool or a large plastic bin filled with play sand or dirt and water, plus your gold nuggets. Use a metal pie pan to scoop up some of the dirt, then swirl the dirt and water around in your pan and look for gold nuggets. Put the nuggets you find in a pouch or a resealable plastic bag.

Famous Folks

Levi Strauss was a German born American who set up a dry goods store in San Francisco in 1853 to sell supplies to the miners. He, along with Jacob Davis, invented riveted work pants. Blue jeans became famous and Strauss died a millionaire.

Additional Layer

In the course of the gold rush the California natives were forced from their land and abused by miners in various ways. Sometimes they were beaten or killed. Many settlers kidnapped Indian women and children and forced them to work as slaves on their plantations. The natives often fought back. This caused retaliation, sometimes official but often vigilante.

Eventually extermination became the official government policy, and a bounty was placed on scalps of native men, women, and children. This is called genocide.

GEOGRAPHY: SOUTHWEST

Arizona, New Mexico, Texas, and Oklahoma are the states known as the Southwest. This part of the country is dry, except for the eastern side of Texas. Most of Arizona, New Mexico, and West Texas are covered in deserts. There are also grasslands, mountains, forests, and swamps. Several major rivers traverse this region, but there are very few natural lakes. Large reservoirs have been built in Texas and Arizona to provide irrigation water and recreation.

This is an old Catholic mission church at Taos Pueblo, New Mexico. It was photographed in 1941 by Ansel Adams. The southwest United States has some of the oldest buildings and settlements in the country. This settlement, though not the church itself, was probably established in about 1200 AD by the Taos Indians who still live in the adobe pueblo buildings. This photograph captures both the influence of the native inhabitants and the Spanish.

The Hopi, Navajo, Comanche, and Apache lived in this region, which was first explored by Coronado in 1540. This land was claimed in the mid 1500s by Spain, the first Spanish settlers being missionaries. Santa Fe, New Mexico is one of the oldest cities in the United States, having been settled in 1608. When Mexico gained its independence from Spain in 1822 the territory became Mexican. Texas, now settled mostly by Americans, revolted from Mexican rule in 1836 and gained their independence as a sovereign nation. They joined the United States by treaty in 1845. In 1848 the United States defeated Mexico in a war and won the southwestern part of what is now the United States.

Oklahoma was designated early in American history as Indian Territory. Many tribes, including the Five Civilized Tribes of the Southeast, were forcibly removed to this area. The territory was supposed to be set aside forever for Native Americans, but by the 1880s white settlers were wanting the prime farmland of the plains, and settlement was opened up in 1889. By 1907 Oklahoma was a state.

During the Civil War these territories and states were Confederate, though New Mexico and Arizona had very little to do with the war. During the early 20th century oil was discovered in Texas, New Mexico, and Oklahoma. The discovery changed the economics of those states forever. Arizona and New Mexico were both made states in 1912. In the 1930s the Dust Bowl catastrophe resulted in major loss of farmland, and people exited Oklahoma and parts of Texas to look for work elsewhere. But the Second World War brought back economic prosperity, especially to New Mexico, which became the testing ground for the new nuclear missile program, receiving billions in federal spending on military installations. During the war Arizona was the site of a German POW (prisoner of war) camp and Japanese-American internment camps.

Since the invention of air conditioning in the 1950s the populations of the southwest deserts has blossomed. Millions of people live or vacation in the southwest during the winter months. The economies of these states are based on technology, military, agriculture, and oil. Texas has the one of the largest economies in the world, on par with Canada and India. Phoenix has boomed over the past few decades until today it has the sixth largest population in America.

☺ ☺ ☻ EXPLORATION: Map of the Southwest
At the end of this unit you will find a map of the southwest to color and label. Use a student atlas to add in the major cities, capitals, rivers, and other natural features. You can also find maps of each individual state from this unit online at www.layers-of-learning.com.

☺ ☺ ☻ EXPLORATION: Bolo Tie
Bolo ties are the official neckware of Texas, Arizona, and New Mexico. They are associated with cowboys and western culture. You can make your own. You will need:

- Decorative flat object (polished stone, wood disk, old piece of costume jewelry, bottle cap, metal end of a belt, etc.)

Fabulous Fact

They say everything is bigger in Texas, but it's actually only the SECOND largest state (trailing Alaska of course). Although, the capitol dome in Austin IS bigger than the U.S. Capitol Building's dome by 7 feet!

Fabulous Fact

The Land Run of 1889 is famous. The territory of Oklahoma was officially opened for settlement, the parcels having been surveyed and marked previously. Hopeful settlers lined up, a gunshot started the race, and thousands of people sped to be the first to claim the choicest parcels of land.

Fabulous Fact

President John F. Kennedy was assassinated while driving through the streets of Dallas in 1963. Immediately controversy ensued about who shot him and whether or not there was some sort of government cover up; the controversy still exists today.

Additional Layer

The clothing worn in a culture is usually related to the lifestyle of the people and their natural environment. How are bolo ties related to the Southwest environment? What other clothing is traditionally southwest, and how does it relate to the lifestyle and environment of the people?

Additional Layer

The Pueblo Indians live in the southwest. They built their homes of adobe and farmed corn and other crops. The Pueblo people include tribes such as the Hopi and the Zuni. Learn more about these people and their way of life.

This photo was taken in the 1890s. It shows a traditional pueblo style blanket, probably woven from wool, which was introduced by the Spanish. Before that the people wove cloth from cotton.

- Bolo tie clips and tips (http://www.bjcraftsupplies.com/bolo/) or you can make your own clip with a picture hanger, bent with pliers into the right shape.
- A piece of cord in leather, hemp, cotton, or plastic. Paracord works well and so do leather boot laces.
- Super glue or jewelry glue.

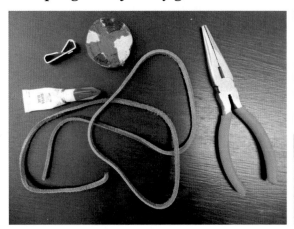

Prepare your decorative piece by removing all hardware, clips, or fabric from the back, leaving a smooth back side. Glue your bolo clip to the back and let the glue dry. Cut your cord to about 36", longer for taller people. When the bolo tie is around your neck it should hang to the bottom of the sternum. Thread the cord through the bolo tie clip. Add decorative tips to the bottom edge of your cord. You can also paint the ends silver if you like.

☺ ☺ ☺ EXPLORATION: Arizona Flag

The Arizona state flag has red and yellow rays, representing the sun and the colors of the Spanish conquistadors who explored and settled the state. There are thirteen rays to represent the thirteen original states. In the center is a copper colored star to represent the state's important copper industry. Finally, the blue on the lower half of the flag represents freedom.

Make your own Arizona flag out of construction paper.

1. Start with a sheet of red as the background.
2. Fold a piece of yellow in half the long way and then find the exact center of the paper. From there, using a ruler, draw the rays from the center point out to the edges. There should be six yellow rays and seven red, spaced more or less equally. Glue the yellow rays onto the red paper.
3. Fold a sheet of blue paper in half the long way, cut it, and glue it to the bottom half of the red sheet.
4. Finally, use a piece of orange paper and cut out a five pointed star. Paste this in the center of the flag.

After you have finished the flag, find facts or information about Arizona and write them on the back side of the flag.

☺ ☺ ☺ EXPLORATION: Grand Canyon

The Grand Canyon is a famous landmark in Arizona. Millions of visitors from all over the world go to see the beautiful sandstone cliffs carved out by the Colorado River. Find the Grand Canyon on a map. Then watch this YouTube video about the canyon from the National Park Service: "Grand Canyon In Depth"

Draw a landscape of the canyon. Start by drawing a squiggly line about one third of the way up your page. Add squiggly oblong and circular shapes above that. Finish the sketch by adding in vertical lines the show the sides of the cliffs. Color the whole thing in desert colors.

On the Web

This short YouTube video shows the landscapes of Arizona: "Arizona From Above - Alien Desert Landscapes"

Fabulous Fact

Besides the Grand Canyon there are many other parks and preserves in Arizona. They include Vermilion Cliffs National Monument, Wupatki and Sunset Crater National Monuments, Montezuma's Castle National Monument, Saguaro National Park, Meteor Crater, Monument Valley, and Petrified Forest National Park.

This is a view inside Saguaro National Park.

Fabulous Fact

Phoenix is the sixth largest city in the United States with more than 1.5 million people. It is situated in the Valley of the Sun, a very dry and hot place. How does a large city in a desert provide water for its people?

On the Web

Watch this video about New Mexico to see the landscape of this state. "New Mexico by Drone in 4K"

Famous Folks

Billy the Kid was a famous cowboy outlaw from New Mexico. He reportedly killed eight men and was a wanted man for most of his short life.

He was killed in a shootout by Sheriff Pat Garrett after escaping jail.

Fabulous Facts

Over a quarter of the people of New Mexico speak Spanish as a first language. Nearly half of the people of New Mexico have Hispanic ancestors, some who are descended from the original Spanish settlers to the area.

☺ ☺ EXPLORATION: Facts About New Mexico

The flag of New Mexico shows the Zia sun symbol of the native peoples. It has four groups of rays with four rays in each group. The number four symbolizes good gifts given by the giver of all good. The good gifts are bound by a circle of love without beginning or end. It is a very old flag, first used by the Spanish for New Mexico in the 1540s.

Cut a piece of yellow construction paper into eight equal pieces. Draw the zia symbol on the back of each paper with a bright red crayon. Then look up information about New Mexico online or in books from the library. Write a different fact on the back of each card.

Use the cards to give an oral report about New Mexico to an audience, like the family or the grandparents.

☺ ☺ EXPLORATION: Albuquerque Balloon Festival

Every year in October Albuquerque, New Mexico sponsors a balloon festival. Thousands of hot air balloons from all over the world fill the skies. Find Albuquerque on a map, then watch this YouTube video about the balloon festival: "Timelapse: Albuquerque Balloon Fiesta".

Finally, design your own balloon to represent something you learned about New Mexico.

Start by cutting four to eight identical balloon shapes from construction paper or card stock in the colors you like. Fold each piece of paper in half, then sketch one half of a balloon shape, making sure the fold is in the center of your design. Cut out the first balloon and use it as a template for the rest of your balloon shapes. You can draw a picture or pattern on each balloon panel if you like. Glue the panels to one another so that they create a single balloon. Add a basket under the balloon with a toilet paper tube, cut down to size. Attach the basket with string or ribbon, and hang the whole balloon.

☺ ☺ ☺ **EXPLORATION: Animal Map**
Hand draw a map of the Southwest region of the United States. Then find out which animals live in each of these states and draw the animals in the locations they live.

Why do the animals live where they do? How do they affect the people who also live in this region?

Fabulous Fact

The roadrunner is a desert bird and the state bird of New Mexico. It walks or runs to catch its prey. It eats snakes, rodents, lizards, insects, and spiders.

Photo by Alan D. Wilson, www.naturespicsonline.com, CC license.

Fabulous Fact

The Carlsbad Caverns of New Mexico are a natural limestone cave system. Over 119 caves were formed when sulfuric acid dissolved the surrounding limestone.

Additional Layer

This is an oil derrick in Texas in 1920.

What kind of impact do you think oil had on the economy and populations of Texas, Oklahoma, and New Mexico? How would those states be different today if oil hadn't been discovered?

Think about the impact one event can have on the history of an area. Have any important events happened in your area to change the course of history?

Fabulous Fact

Texas is known as the Lone Star State because of the flag of Texas.

The star standing by itself represents Texan independence. You can see the Texas flag flying proudly all over Texas.

☺ EXPLORATION: Texas Regions

Texas can be divided into regions. Read about the different regions of Texas on this website: https://tpwd.texas.gov/education/kids/about-texas/regions/texas-regions-for-big-kids

Choose one of the regions and create a brochure that convinces people to visit this part of Texas. You may need to do further research to learn more about the attractions of Texas.

You can create your own, or you can use a printable brochure template from Layers-of-Learning.com.

☺ ☺ ☺ EXPLORATION: Texas Landscape Map

Hand draw a map of Texas, using a student atlas for reference. On the map, mark the locations of major cities and landmarks. Color the map to show the different types of landscapes in various parts of Texas, from the mountains in the Big Bend region to the plains in the panhandle and the swamps along the Louisiana border. Include a compass rose, a title, and a key.

☺ ☺ EXPLORATION: Economics of the Southwest

At the end of this unit you will find an "Economics of the Southwest" printable. Color the sheet. Do some research and find out the major industries, energy productions and uses, and agriculture for the Southwest region. Write the information in the boxes. Cut out the big arm of the oil derrick along with the upper part of the sheet, above the drawings and words. Glue the cut out sheet to a background paper. Attach the oil derrick arm to the oil rig with a brad so the arm can move up and down.

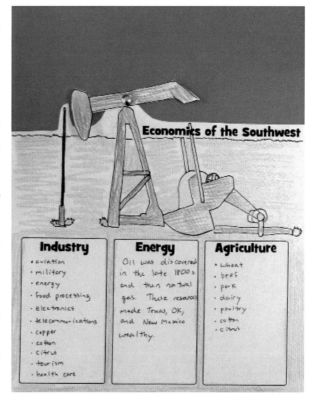

☺ ☺ ☺ EXPLORATION: Oklahoma

Draw a map of Oklahoma. Put in the rivers and mountains. Use color coding to show the landscape types (desert, grassland, mountains, etc.) Then add in the major cities. Finally, add some symbols that show how the land is being used. For example, you might have a symbol to show wheat farming, one to show cattle farming, and one to show where oil is harvested. Does it make sense to you that each of the human activities on your map is connected to the landscape?

☺ ☻ EXPLORATION: Southwest Fact Sheet

At the end of this unit you will find a printable of cutouts to glue to a fact sheet about the southwest region. Color the pictures, cut them out on the dashed lines, then glue or tape one edge to another sheet of paper or card stock so that the pictures create flaps. Under each flap write information in the flap's category. For example, under the "people" flap you might tell the percentages of languages spoken in the region. You might tell how many of the people in the region live in cities and how many live in small towns or rural areas. You might tell about an important festival or industry in the region. You can write a sentence or two or make a bulleted list. These can also be used as components in a lapbook or notebooking page if you're keeping one during your state studies.

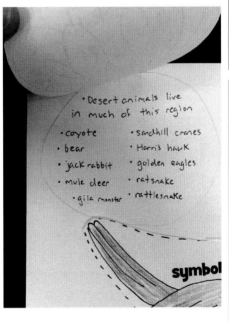

☺ ☻ ☻ EXPLORATION: Route 66

Route 66, one of the earliest highways in the U.S. system runs through all four of the states in this unit. Find Route 66 on a map. Learn more about some of the towns it passes through. Make an illustrated highway map of your own, featuring the sights along the way.

Fabulous Fact

Oklahoma was Indian Territory in early United States history. The Southwest tribes were forcibly moved there in the 1830s. After slavery ended, black settlers moved in droves to the territory. Today Oklahoma still has very large populations of Native Americans and African Americans.

Additional Layer

Major traffic routes like Route 66 support communities because of the traffic that passes through them. In 1985 Route 66 was officially retired from the federal highway system and replaced with interstates, thus killing many towns along the route. Think about how the placement of roads and railroads has determined the locations of towns. It is very much the same as cities that grow up along rivers. It's all about transport.

SCIENCE: EARTH STRUCTURE

Earth is not just a solid ball of rock with random big basins where water gathers. Earth is complex and layered. The outside of the earth is called the crust. It's the part we see, stand on, dig holes in, and live on. It is the surface of the earth. But under the surface, Earth isn't so friendly. Beneath the crust there is molten rock, really hot rock, more really hot rock, and then a solid core of metal.

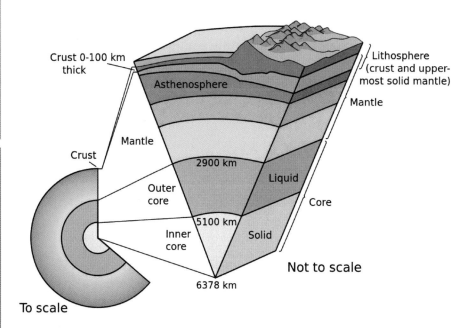

The way the earth is structured is very important. The structure of the earth allows it to create magnetic fields which protect us from the sun and objects in space, produce new rock (including minerals and gases that we use on a regular basis), act as a vast recycling plant of air, water, rock, soil, and everything else. This recycling feature means it can repair and heal itself. Besides that, understanding the structure of the earth helps us understand and, partially at least, predict earthquakes and volcanoes. Deep down under the crust are all the materials we need to not just survive, but thrive, and they are there in such incredible abundance. It is largely because of what goes on beneath the surface that the earth is called a living planet. It is a changing, dynamic, regenerating place, so unlike the deadness and cold hostility of the moon.

☺ ☻ **EXPLORATION: Color a Diagram of Earth's Layers**
Some questions about the earth's layers may have occurred to you. Why would some of the layers, or zones within the layers, be liquid and others solid? We do know that all the layers of the inside of the earth are very, very hot, hence the melting of rock and

metal. But then why would some of it not be melted? Our best guess is the intense pressure. As pressure builds, the temperature needed to melt the rock or metal would increase, so deeper layers under more pressure would still be solid. The images of the earth's internal structure make it look very neat and tidy, with perfectly spherical and smooth layers, but it's not really that way. In reality it would be messier than that, with hot pockets and cooler pockets, molten bits and more solid bits, and some bits halfway in between.

At the end of this unit you will find a printable diagram of earth's layers to color.

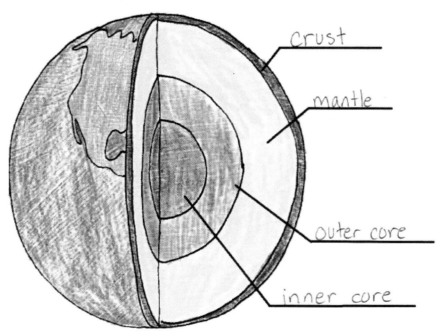

☺ ☻ EXPLORATION: Detailed Diagram of Earth's Guts

The diagram on the next page is much more detailed for older kids who already have learned about the basics. Print out a copy from the end of this unit. There are several ways of thinking about the layers of the earth. You can think of it in terms of rheological properties (physical characteristics like liquid or solid), in terms of chemical properties, or in terms of mathematical physics of waves passing through the earth. The diagram we created includes aspects of all three.

The major layers - crust, mantle, and core - are chemical layers. Each has a very different composition of predominant elements. The viscosity, or state of melt, in each layer further divides it.

On The Web

Watch Khan Academy on the structure of the earth. https://www.khanacademy.org/science/cosmology-and-astronomy/earth-history-topic/plate-techtonics/v/structure-of-the-earth

Look at the menu on the left side of the screen to watch other related videos about plate tectonics and earth structure for this and the next unit, Unit 4-7.

Famous Folks

In 1936 a Danish geophysicist and mathematician named Inge Lehmann discovered the solid inner core and the molten outer core of the earth.

She carefully and mathematically analyzed the data from earthquakes and realized that the entire inner parts of the earth could not be one single molten mass.

Photo from OI-i.lavin, CC licence , Wikimeida

Fabulous Fact

On the worksheet to the right we talk about the lithosphere being made up of silicates. Silicates are minerals that are composed of silicon and oxygen. 90% of the rocks in the earth's crust are based on silicates. Minerals like topaz, horneblende, talc, biotite, quartz, and emerald, and dozens of others begin with a silicon and oxygen base. For example, the mineral zircon has a formula of $ZrSiO_4$.

The other 10% of the earth's crust is made of things like iron, gold, silver, platinum, rare earth elements, carbon, copper, arsenic, and their compounds.

On the Web

This pdf goes into much more detail about the evidence for the internal structure of the earth: http://www.tcd.ie/Geology/assets/pdf/geology-for-engineers/L02_mantle.pdf

Have your high school student read it.

The boundaries between layers - Moho, Gutenberg, and Lehmann-Bullen - are places where seismic waves change direction and can be calculated for mathematically.

Have the kids read the descriptions of each of the layers and then match the letter to the description. In the colored diagram below we give the answers.

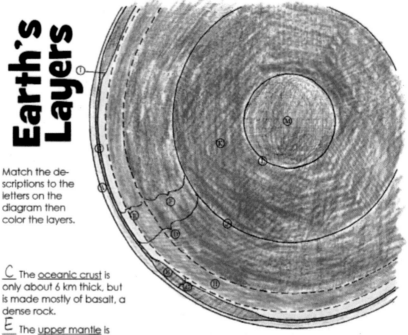

Earth's Layers

Match the descriptions to the letters on the diagram then color the layers.

C The oceanic crust is only about 6 km thick, but is made mostly of basalt, a dense rock.

E The upper mantle is a very viscous melted, or plastic, rock.

J The Gutenberg discontinuity is the boundary between the mantle and outer core.

A The outermost layer of the earth is completely gas. It is called the atmosphere.

G The upper layer of the upper mantle is cooler and is solid rock, this combined with the crust is the lithosphere. The lithosphere is made mostly of silicates.

M The inner core is also made of iron and nickel, but is under enough pressure to be mostly solid.

B The continental crust is thick, an average of 35 km, but is made mostly of granite and is less dense than the oceanic crust.

D The mantle is the thickest layer and makes up the bulk of the earth. It is divided into several regions.

H The lower part of the upper mantle is called the asthenosphere.

L The Lehmann-Bullen discontinuity is the boundary between the inner and outer cores.

I The Mohorovicic discontinuity is the boundary between the mantle and the crust.

F The lower mantle is very very hot, but is under pressure so it is more viscous than the upper mantle.

K The outer core is made of iron and nickel and is molten metal.

☺ ☻ ☺ EXPERIMENT: How Do We Know?

The evidence for the internal structure of the earth comes mostly from the seismic waves of earthquakes. Seismic waves are sound waves created by an earthquake and passed through rock. Seismometers, sensitive instruments that can detect and record seismic waves, are placed all over the earth. Earthquakes are also happening almost all of the time somewhere on the earth. Scientists compare the time a particular earthquake's waves are recorded by a seismometer to the time the earthquake actually took place. That tells them how fast the waves passed through the earth. Sound waves pass through different materials at different speeds. This helps us know what materials the inside of the earth is made of. When sound waves change speed they also change direction. Seismometers can also be used to find these directional changes, helping us learn the density and thickness of the inner layers of the earth. Further, something in the center of the earth deflects or blocks sound waves from passing through that point, so we know something very solid and dense is in the center. This diagram shows how the waves pass through the earth and are deflected or blocked.

Fabulous Fact

Scientists have calculated the overall density of the earth based on its velocity and volume. That density is much larger than the density of the rocks in the crust of the earth, so there must be some very dense inner layers to the earth to make up the difference.

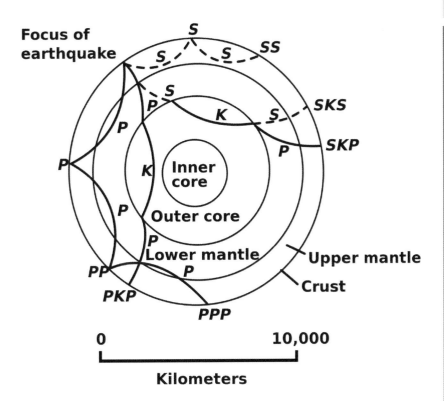

P-waves are primary waves, or the first waves that are recorded from an earthquake. They pass through denser materials more quickly than they pass through less dense materials. You can test this for yourself.

You will need a string and some tape. Cut a piece of string about 2 feet long. Tape one end of the string to a table or countertop. You might need someone to hold the string and tape in place. Stretch the string taut and flick it with your finger to create noise. Then wrap the loose end (the end

Additional Layer

Between the layers of the earth are boundaries called "discontinuities." These are places where the seismic velocities actually change. There is something really there, not just a boundary line on paper.

The Mohorovicic Discontinuity, or Moho, is thought to be a place where the composition changes from feldspar rocks above to non-feldspar rocks below. So besides differences in temperature and viscosity, there are differences in chemical composition between the various layers of the earth.

Watch this YouTube video about the Moho:

"The mohorovicic seismic discontinuity" from Khan Academy.

Additional Layer

Plastic bags are one of the worst pollutants in the world's oceans and often cause the deaths of sea creatures that can mistake them for food. But melted down plastic lumps would not endanger sea creatures.

This is a photo by the NOAA of a beach in Hawaii. Plastic trash from all over the world, collected in the ocean, has been washed ashore.

Additional Layer

We have very blithely told you that the inner core of the earth is a solid, but the truth is we only know that it *acts* like a solid, deflecting the seismic waves as it does.

As we speak, scientists are hard at work trying to figure out what the core really is. Is it a plasma under huge pressure? Go read all about it.

not taped to the table) around your pointer finger and insert your finger into your ear. Flick the string again. The sound is much louder now. The first time the sound was passing through air to your ear. The second time it was passing through the solid string to your ear. Waves passing through different materials have different effects that can be detected.

☺ ☺ ☺ EXPERIMENT: Plastic Planet

The insides of the earth, the molten lava, isn't really liquid, but it isn't entirely solid. It's a state of matter we call plastic - or in other words, the rock has developed plasticity because of the high temperature it is at.

Everyone knows what plastic is, the material, I mean. Plastic is called "plastic" because when it is warm it is liquidy, not quite runny like water, but fluid and moldable. Rock and metal do the same thing, but at much higher temperatures than plastic. We'll use plastic grocery bags to demonstrate plasticity.

WARNING: This experiment will use high heat, so an adult or teen should do the actual experiment while younger kids observe.

You need plastic grocery bags, a saucepan, a metal "tin" can, cooking oil, and a stove or hot plate.

1. Fill the saucepan about half full of oil and place on the stove; set the heat at a medium temperature.
2. Stuff several plastic bags into the can, and place the can into the oil.
3. Allow it to heat and melt the plastic. If the oil begins to smoke, it's way too hot; pull it off the burner and let it cool.
4. Use tongs to grab the can with melted plastic and pull it out, setting it on another heat resistant surface. It will still be very, very hot. Warn the kids not to touch the can or the oil dripping from it.
5. Poke and prod the plastic. Once it has cooled a little, dump it out on a paper plate and let the kids poke and prod it with a stick to get a feel for the viscosity and moldability. This is how the melted rock and metal under the earth would be, not liquid, but not solid either.

P.S. Your oil is still good and can be used as long as you didn't spill plastic into it.

☺ ☺ ☺ EXPERIMENT: Wobbly Planet

Way back in Year One when we were studying astronomy we learned that the earth wobbles a bit on its axis (Unit 1-3 Experiment: Precession). The star above the North Pole moves over time, or more accurately, the North Pole of the earth moves as the earth wobbles. The theory is that this wobbling occurs because the inside of the earth is not a solid, but is at least partially a viscous liquid. To see how this works you need two eggs, one boiled and one raw.

Spin the two eggs. Compare the movement of the raw egg to the boiled egg. The raw egg wobbles more and slows down much more quickly than the boiled egg, which has a solid center.

Remember that according to Newton's Laws of Motion an object at rest wants to stay at rest; it has inertia. Because the inner part of the earth is liquid enough to flow, it can spin at a different rate and exert forces contrary to the overriding force of the earth's orbit, throwing the whole thing off just a little.

☺ ☺ ☻ EXPERIMENT: Layers
So why does the earth form into layers at all?

Throw chopped carrots into a pot of water; they sink. Boil the water; the carrots rise. Add corn starch, thicken it, and let it cool. Dump out the solid stuff and cut through the layers. Where are the carrots? Try this with more materials of different densities.

Different materials with different densities and at different temperatures move to different places because of gravity. Heavier, denser things move toward the center of the earth while lighter things are left closer to the surface.

☺ ☺ ☻ EXPERIMENT: Earth's Magnetic Field
We know Earth has a magnetic field, but why? Where does the magnetic field come from, and how is it maintained? The theory is that because the insides of the earth are not solid, they move. This movement causes moving electrons, and moving electrons can create a magnetic field. This theory is called the dynamo theory.

Teaching Tip

A boiled egg makes a good visual representation of the earth. The shell is like the crust. Break it up a bit to see it crack into "plates." The white is like the mantle and the yolk is like the core.

You can also create models out of play dough in various colors.

Famous Folks

Francis Birch was an American geophysicist who built on the work of Lehmann to discover the chemical composition of the layers of the earth. It was he who determined that the mantle was made of silicates and the core was most likely iron.

Fabulous Fact

In what appears to be complete randomness, the direction of the magnetic field can suddenly reverse, flopping the north and south poles. Evidence for reversed magnetic poles can be found in basalt of the sea floor, where metallic minerals line up north to south (or south to north as the case may be). None of these flops have occurred during human history, but you never know, maybe this will be our lucky year.

On the Web

Just like the inside of the earth isn't static, neither is its magnetic field. Read this article that explains how the field changes constantly: http://earthsky.org/earth/how-earths-magnetic-field-is-changing-swarm

Fabulous Fact

The Coriolis effect also explains why tropical storms always rotate counterclockwise in the northern hemisphere and clockwise in the south. It can be terribly mathematical if you're interested in that sort of thing, a sort of melding of earth science and physics.

Get some iron filings and a magnet to see how the magnetic field of the earth would look if you could see it.

We got this self-contained package of iron filings from Home Science Tools.

The portion of the earth that is thought to cause this magnetic field is the molten outer core, which is made of metal (which if you will recall means flowing electrons) and is liquid enough for the whole thing to be flowing. Remember making an electromagnet in Unit 2-20? Flowing electrons can create a magnetic field. Ta da! Earth has an awesomely massive layer of flowing metal, which made it possible for Columbus to find the Americas and for all of our compasses to work.

Okay, but why does the molten metal flow? Because of the Coriolis effect. The Coriolis effect predicts that objects (in this case flowing metal) will be deflected in a circular pattern. The earth is spinning. Because the earth is spinning there is a force created that tends to throw loose objects off; we call that a centrifugal force (like a kid on a spinning merry-go-round at a playground). But because the earth is spinning in a circle, the loose stuff can't fly straight off; it's deflected in a circle. (Have you ever seen a kid fly off a spinning merry-go-round? Aside from the crying, there is the fascinating fact that they don't fly off in a straight line.) And in fact, on the earth the object doesn't fly off at all because the force of gravity keeps it all together, but the spinning does cause the liquid metal to flow. Here's one concept of how the molten metal in the earth's core might be flowing and creating a magnetic field.

☺ ☻ EXPLORATION: Hot Earth

Earth scientists and physicists have several beliefs about why the inside of the earth is hot. First, we assume that during the formation of the earth (and the moon and other planets) all of the material was hot and molten, so we had a start of great temperatures.

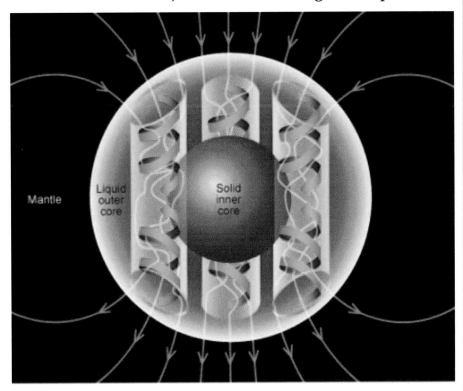

Mantle — Liquid outer core — Solid inner core

But why didn't the earth cool and harden clear through like the moon? It would take the earth quite a bit longer to cool than the moon because the earth is larger by quite a bit. In fact, early estimates of the age of the earth were based on the temperature of the inside of the earth and the rate of cooling that could be expected.

But then astrophysicists came up with much longer dates for the age of the earth based on the movement of stars and expansion of the universe. The earth by those estimates should be a cold dead rock by now.

So there are a couple of reasons why the earth is still hot. First, there's friction. The movement of rocks sliding against rocks inside the earth creates heat, and that heat is enough to keep things pretty warm, especially near the surface where plates are sliding and grinding and in the core where the molten metal swirls.

Try this:
1. Get a clean, empty soda pop bottle with a narrow neck and put it into the freezer for about twenty minutes.
2. Cut out a circle of cardboard or card stock just larger than the

Additional Layer

Since the earth's outer core is not rigidly connected to the mantle, some scientists think that the core may be rotating at a different rate from the rest of the planet.

They use the seismology readings and magnetic field to study the possibility.

Sometimes when reading science books, especially text books, it can seem like there are no new questions, only answers already given (which need to be reproduced on a test).

As you read about the structure of the earth look for the questions scientists still have.

Additional Layer

The interiors of the other rocky planets in the solar system are probably very similar to Earth's layers. We know they have volcanoes, for example. This is the inside of Venus.

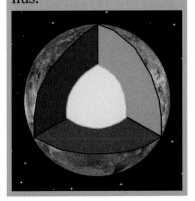

Additional Layer

Felsic lava, which forms continental granite rock, occurs when continental rock is melted into the mafic lava already under the earth, increasing its silica levels. The other rocky planets in our solar system have crusts made of basalt, like Earth's oceans. Without our continental rock the whole earth would be ocean. So how did the continental rock form in the first place if new continental rock always starts out with old continental rock?

This article documents a team of scientists who studied the isthmus of Panama and found "juvenile continental crust."

http://phys.org/news/2015-03-scientists-elusive-secret-continents.html

Explanation

In Unit 3-11 we delved deeply into the different types of igneous rocks and how they are formed, including the differences between felsic and mafic rocks.

Mafic lava is much runnier than felsic lava because mafic has a lot less silica in it.

opening of the bottle.

3. Take the bottle out of the freezer and place the circle of cardboard over the neck.
4. Rub your hands vigorously together until you can feel the heat from the friction.
5. Place your hands around the cold bottle and watch as the circle of cardboard lifts and pops repeatedly as the air molecules, warmed from the heat, leave the bottle.

The biggest reason for the continued heat of the earth though, is that there are chemical reactions involving radioactive material, which gives off heat as it decays. This keeps the earth hot for a long time, long after it theoretically should have cooled.

☺ ☺ ☺ EXPLORATION: Two Types of Crust

The earth's crust is made up of two different types of material. One is continental crust, which is made of felsic rock which forms all sorts of igneous rocks and then transforms into sedimentary or metamorphic rock. The other is oceanic crust, which is made of mafic rock which forms into either basalt or gabbro. Continental crust is much thicker and older than oceanic crust. Oceanic crust is much denser than continental crust. Because oceanic crust is thinner and denser than continental crust, it sinks lower into the molten layers of earth below it and forms the deep basins that are the oceans.

Look up more information on the earth's crust. Make a table of facts comparing the oceanic and continental crust. It should look kind of like this:

Crust	Thick-ness	Density	Compo-sition	Rock Types
Oceanic				
Continental				

Then make a model of the oceanic and continental crust with play dough or salt dough. Use two colors, one for the oceanic crust and one for the continental crust. Be able to explain the two types of crust and how they are different.

☺ ☺ ☺ EXPLORATION: Convection Cells

The center is the hottest part of the earth, and it heats the liquid mantle above it, like a stove heats a pot of water. The heat rises toward the surface and then falls again as it cools. This creates a current called a convection current. The convec-

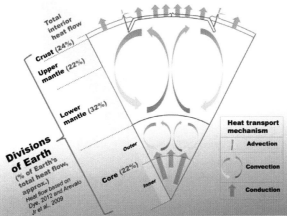

Image by Bkilli1, CC license, Wikimedia

tion cells in the mantel refine and separate the minerals in the earth's core into felsic and mafic rock compositions, making the oceanic and continental crusts.

You can watch this process with some glitter, oil, a stove, and a pot. Just pour a little glitter into the bottom of a small sauce pan. Then fill the pan ¾ or so full of cooking oil. Turn the heat on medium. As the oil heats, the pieces of glitter get carried to the surface on currents. Then as they cool, they settle back down again.

Deep Thoughts

What if there weren't two different types of crust, but only one? How would Earth be different?

Fabulous Fact

The convection cell description and graphic to the left explain the theory of "whole mantle convection." Not all scientists agree with this. Some say the heat is carried up in plumes from the core and then much smaller, closer to the surface convection cells occur.

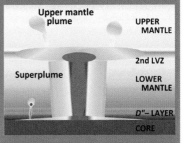

Image by Brews ohare, CC license Wikimedia.

Additional Layer

People create models and experiments of things we can't possibly observe first-hand, like the inner workings of Earth. This works because the principles of physics are constant. This idea, that the Laws of the Universe are unchanging, is called uniformitarianism. But while the laws of nature do not change, the rate of processes may change. It's still being debated.

THE ARTS: IMPRESSIONISM II

Teaching Tip

Unit 4-5 includes a section on Impressionism I that discusses the characteristics of Impressionist paintings. This is a continuation of that unit and deals with the individual artists who were part of that movement. Use the units together for a more complete look at Impressionism.

Famous Folks

Charles Glyre was the teacher of three of the masters of Impressionism - Monet, Renoir, and Sisley. Their style did not evolve from him necessarily, but the three became friends and spent summers painting together in the forest nearby. Gleyre taught them all at the Ecole des Beaux-Arts.

The first Impressionists were bold and daring. They were a group of friends who socialized together and painted together, swapping ideas and emboldening each other to create in their own way instead of in the traditional style being taught in Paris art schools. They challenged the established and accepted norms of painting by introducing new colors, light, and modern scenes to painting. They threw out the idea that you had to paint with slow precision and instead focused on painting moments, impressions, to be lived and enjoyed. They painted outdoors, used quick brush strokes, and let the beauty of moments in real life shine through.

Rejected by the Paris Salon, they created their own exhibition where they showed and sold their paintings. They had difficulty selling anything, but eventually several art dealers took a liking to their work and began buying it to sell to consumers. The style eventually caught on, especially in America. It took quite awhile before they were accepted in the art world, but in the end they changed the face of art and brought in a new style - modern art.

☺ ☻ **EXPLORATION: Monet's Water Lilies**

Claude Monet was the quintessential Impressionist. He captured light, painted in bright, pure colors, and focused on the impressions of scenes rather than precise details. He loved to paint outdoors and made many versions of his favorite scenes.

He bought a home in Giverny and transformed the gardens. He built a pond with a Japanese footbridge, imported and planted many beautiful plants and flowers, and created a Japanese garden. He spent his last thirty years gardening and painting. He painted around 250 pictures of the water lilies he had planted in his pond. He was fascinated with the light and the reflections on the water's surface.

Make your own water lilies art using layered tissue paper. Begin with turquoise blue card stock. Brush a thin layer of white glue all over it. Layer torn pieces of lavender and blue tissue paper to cover the paper and create the look of the water in the pond. Cut out lily pads from light green card stock and paste them on around the pond. Crinkle up white tissue paper circles and glue on to the lily pads to create the flowers. Finally, add torn little, yellow tissue paper centers to the flowers. Don't worry about perfect, neat edges. Monet's paintings were rough and textured, and there were very few distinct lines anywhere.

☺ ☻ EXPLORATION: Auguste Renoir

Auguste Renoir got his first job as a plate designer at a porcelain factory. He was a talented artist and expanded his skills while studying at the Louvre. He painted throughout his entire life, even strapping a paintbrush on to his hand when his arthritis became so bad that he could no longer hold the brush on his own.

He liked to paint joyful, pretty pictures. He once said, "For me a picture should be a pleasant thing, joyful and pretty - yes, pretty!" Parties, dances, and social gatherings in Paris and in the surrounding countryside were his favorite subjects. Rather than nature, he focused on people in his paintings, although the scenes still tended to be outdoors.

Watch this Smarthistory video about Renoir's Luncheon of the Boating Party for a comparison of this and other paintings, as well as some interesting insights about the painting: https://youtu.be/feCG2zfzflo.

☺ ☻ ☻ EXPLORATION: Alfred Sisley Study

Alfred Sisley was a Paris native with British parents. He met the other Impressionist painters while studying with Charles Glyre. He associated with them and stayed friends throughout his life, painting, socializing, and exhibiting his art. He painted landscapes in soft, tranquil colors. He had trouble selling his paintings though and was poor his whole life, but after he died his art became much more appreciated.

Additional Layer

The Louvre in Paris was more than just a museum. Painters came to the Louvre to train under masters and learn the techniques of painting. They copied the works of centuries of famous artists. Training was rigorous and students were expected to focus on Biblical and historical subjects, not modern scenes and everyday life.

When the Impressionists rejected the traditional style and techniques, they also rejected the traditional subject matter. Everything they did was an affront to the traditional thoughts about what art should be.

The Louvre is the largest museum in the world. Today there is a small, obscure section of the Louvre dedicated to the paintings of the Impressionists, but you have to go to the Musee d'Orsay or other Impressionist museums to see most of their collections in Paris.

Famous Folks

Paul Durand-Ruel was an art dealer who brought Impressionism to the United States.

He opened an art gallery on Fifth Avenue in New York City and held an exhibition highlighting the new style. Americans loved the style and it became much more popular than it had been in Paris. He also brought it to England and sold paintings out of his London gallery.

This portrait of him was done by Renoir.

Fabulous Fact

The Impressionist Exhibitions lasted from 1874 to 1886. The shows stopped after that, but the style lived on and evolved as other artists continued to develop Impressionist themes and ideas.

If you look at several of Sisley's paintings you'll quickly be able to pick out his style.

Create your own version of a Sisley by trying to copy this painting, "Paysage avec maisons" (Landscape with houses), in your sketchbook or on a canvas. Get a variety of brushes to work with so you can play with the quick brush strokes of different sizes and shapes of brushes. Notice that his brush strokes on the ground tend to be horizontal while his brush strokes in the sky above tend to be vertical. Try to make yours look as much like Sisley's as you can. When the Impressionist painters studied painting, they spent years copying paintings of famous painters to practice their techniques and perfect their work. They didn't begin to paint quickly until after they had studied and honed their skills.

☺ ☺ ☺ EXPLORATION: Frederic Bazille's Family

Frederic Bazille began painting full time after flunking out of medical school. He was already friends with some of the Impressionists. He joined the military when the Franco-Prussian War broke out and was killed in battle at age 28. He painted some beautiful paintings first though. He liked to paint people with lovely landscapes in the background.

Bazille often painted people he knew, from fellow artists to members of his family. He made a group portrait of his family called "Family Reunion" that is his most famous painting. It was actually accepted at the Salon in Paris, perhaps because he painted in a more refined style than many Impressionists. Still, he painted en plein air and focused on light and colorful natural scenes rather than historical paintings.

Make your own family reunion sketch in your sketchbook. Draw each member of your family in a natural setting.

☺ ☺ ☺ EXPLORATION: Pissarro's Palette

Camille Pissarro was the oldest of the group of Impressionist painters. Many of them saw him almost as a father figure among the group. He was a mentor to many of the younger artists. He continued the trend of Impressionist painters by going against artistic norms of the time and breaking the rules of formality. At times he skipped the canvas altogether, instead painting directly on his palette from the leftover blobs of paint.

Use the printable paint palette to make your own palette painting. You can print it on to thick paper or use it as a template to cut out a palette shape using wood.

Begin by putting blobs of paint on your palette as though you were preparing to paint a picture. Instead of using a canvas, use your brushes to swirl and move the paint on the palette itself, creating a scene directly on the palette like Pisarro did. This is his palette, complete with a painting of a cart and peasants.

Famous Folks

Felix Nadar was a famous Parisian photographer. He was the first aerial photographer to take pictures of Paris from a hot air balloon. Friends with many of the Impressionist painters, he even hosted their very first exhibition.

Fabulous Fact

Not only did the Impressionists have the benefit of portable paint tubes, but they also had new colors. New, brightly colored pigments had been created and they utilized them. Instead of the brown paintings with dark shadows that were popular at the time, they painted brightly colored and well lit everyday scenes with blue and violet shadows. Their paintings were full of light.

Additional Layer

Most of the Impressionist painters had cameras. They dabbled in photography as well as painting. They noticed that in the pictures some parts in the background seemed out of focus, almost fuzzy. Sometimes the whole picture even turned out a bit fuzzy.

They developed painting techniques based on those pictures. They also experimented with cropping and with perspective. They could change the camera angle or position and completely change the photograph. Likewise, they could do the same things with their paintings.

The invention of the camera had a definite impact on Impressionist style. Since a camera could easily capture a likeness; they wanted their paintings to capture the feeling of a moment instead.

Memorization Station

Memorize some of the categories of paintings.

Portraits =
paintings of people

Land/sea/cityscapes =
paintings of places

Still lifes =
paintings of things

☺ ☺ ☺ EXPLORATION: Setting Manet's Scene

Edouard Manet was born into a wealthy family in Paris who had great plans for him to become a lawyer. He wanted to be an artist though, so he went to the Louvre to study painting. He made many paintings in the Impressionist style, and definitely shirked the traditional, accepted ways of painting, but he never actually exhibited with the Impressionists in Paris. He continually submitted his work to the Salon and was often rejected. He didn't really become accepted as an artist until much later in his life.

He painted this young man playing the fife based on a soldier in a Spanish regiment. It was criticized harshly because of the monochromatic background that doesn't allow us to know the surroundings or the relative size or importance of the fifer. After it was rejected by the Salon, Manet paid to hold his own exhibit; it was further criticized there.

Print the outline picture of *The Fifer* from the printables section. Color him in and then draw in your own background that helps tell more of the story about who your fifer is.

☺ ☺ EXPLORATION: Still Life With Cezanne

Paul Cezanne liked to paint still life paintings. He saw geometric shapes in the things he painted, and especially appreciated the shapes of simple things like fruit.

Look at several of his apple still life paintings on the internet or in an art book. Now make your own. You'll need thick watercolor paper, oil pastels, watercolor paints, and brushes.

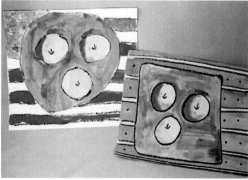

Begin by drawing 3 or 4 small circles on your paper in pencil, then outlining them in oil pastel; these are your apples. Now add a large circle or square that surrounds all of the smaller circles; this is your plate. Again, outline it in oil pastel. Add a small U with a line coming up from it to create your stems using oil pastels. Now paint one side of each of your apples. You can use green, red, or yellow. Paint the rest of your apples yellow. Use a bit more of the reds, greens, and yellows to blend the colors of each of your apples. Let them dry.

Now paint your bowl a solid color. Carefully paint around your apples so the colors don't mix.

Design your tablecloth using any combination of colors and patterns that you like with paints and color pastels.

☺ ☺ ☺ EXPLORATION: Morisot's Candid Paintings

Berthe Morisot was the only woman to take part in the very first Impressionist Exhibition. Before that exhibition her paintings had been shown at six Salon Exhibitions in a row. She was accomplished and well-known. When she joined with the Impressionists she decided to join in their exhibitions rather than showing at the Salon again.

She was friends with many of the Impressionist painters and eventually married Edouard Manet's brother, Eugene. She painted her own experiences, which were mostly scenes of women and children. Rather than creating formal portraits, she painted real, everyday scenes that she experienced. They feel more like candid shots than formal portraits.

Use a camera and take a series of pictures. First, choose a subject and help them pose for several formal shots. Make sure they are facing the camera and are perfectly posed with a well-composed background and perfect lighting. Once you've taken several formal photos, take candid pictures of the same subject. This time, just have them go about their normal activities. Write about the differences between the two series of photographs.

Writer's Workshop

The Impressionist painters were not just people who painted in the same style. They were friends. They hung out together, especially at the Cafe Guerbois, where they talked about art and literature, relaxed, and shared a meal.

Write about what you like to do with your friends. Do they inspire you and give you ideas?

Fabulous Fact

Traditional portraits had been formal and posed. With the invention of the camera, people began to be portrayed more candidly. Impressionists took to this new candid style and began to paint casual, everyday portraits of people doing all sorts of things. They painted everyday moments in the lives of their subjects. They didn't worry about poses or perfect features, but rather just captured the moments the people were experiencing.

Fabulous Fact

Degas liked to paint in his studio, but most Impressionists took advantage of the city's brand new trains. Resort towns sprung up near Paris and were only a train ride away and made for pleasing scenes to paint.

Additional Layer

Some of the Impressionists were also inspired by the Japanese art that had come to Paris during the World's Fair. Degas began collecting art from Japan. Monet even built a Japanese garden with a Japanese style footbridge at his home so he could paint scenes from his garden. This was the same bridge he painted many times in his water lilies paintings. Monet painted his wife in Japanese attire as well.

☺ ☻ EXPLORATION: Dancers and Degas

Edgar Degas painted in the Impressionist style and socialized with that whole group of painters, but he called himself a Realist. He wasn't as spontaneous or quick with his paintings. He planned, thought through, and worked on his paintings. He rejected en plein air painting as well, preferring to paint in a studio. Despite this, he painted contemporary scenes that felt like he had captured a moment. His brushstrokes were visible and he mixed colors using a combination of pigments right on the canvas, just as other Impressionists did. He focused on movement as much as Monet focused on light. Most of his paintings were of ballerinas, sometimes performing, but also in class, resting, or practicing.

Make your own ballerina art. Start by dying a coffee filter. Drop water, colored with food dye, from an eye-dropper, all over the coffee filter. While the coffee filter dries, draw a ballerina. Size your drawing so that the coffee filter folded in half will be the right scale to become her skirt. Once you've drawn your ballerina and her background setting and the coffee filter is dry, fold the colorful coffee filter in half. Layer other unpainted coffee filters as an underskirt, and attach the layers of the ballerina's skirt using glue at the waistband.

☺ ☻ EXPLORATION: Cassatt's Japan-Inspired Art

In 1867 the World's Fair came to Paris. This was the same fair the Eiffel Tower was built for. During the fair there were things on display from all around the world, but the Japanese art was a standout. Soon Japanese influences were found in European art. Fans, kimonos, and vases were included as props. The simple Japanese style with pure colors, no shadows, and asymmetry became part of European paintings.

Mary Cassatt was particularly smitten by the simple Japanese style. She was an American who had come to Paris to study the paintings of the old masters. While in Paris she discovered the paintings of Degas and said her life was changed by them. The two became lifelong friends. Like Degas, she did not call herself an Impressionist. She always referred to the close-knit group of painters as "Independents."

Mary made many Japanese style prints using woodcuts. She etched her design into wood, applied paint, and then pressed paper on it to create a print. She could use the same woodcut over and over to make copies of her paintings. You can make your own by carving your picture into a piece of flat styrofoam. Paint the foam using acrylic paints, but be careful not to get paint into the cracks you've carved. You'll need to work quickly so your paint doesn't dry. Then press your paper down on the foam and lift it up carefully. Let your print dry.

Famous Folks
Cassatt was an active and outspoken women's suffragist. She had gone beyond most women in the art world and was not afraid to stand up for women's rights.

On the Web
Impressionism spread to America before long. Cassatt was the first American to embrace it, but soon Whistler, Homer, Tanner, Eakins, and others were all joining the movement. Go visit the Met's American Impression website to learn more: http://www.met-museum.org/toah/hd/aimp/hd_aimp.htm

Coming up next . . .
Unit 4-7

Civil War
National Parks
Plate Tectonics
Post-Impressionism

My ideas for this unit:

Title: _____ **Topic:** _____

_____

_____

_____

_____

_____

_____

_____

_____

_____

_____

Title: _____ **Topic:** _____

_____

_____

_____

_____

_____

_____

_____

_____

_____

_____

_____

Title: _____ **Topic:** _____

_____

_____

_____

_____

_____

_____

_____

_____

_____

_____

Title: _____ **Topic:** _____

_____

_____

_____

_____

_____

_____

_____

_____

_____

_____

Title: _____ **Topic:** _____

_____

_____

_____

_____

_____

_____

_____

_____

_____

_____

Title: _____ **Topic:** _____

_____

_____

_____

_____

_____

_____

_____

_____

_____

_____

Moving Out West

The Louisiana Purchase doubled the size of the United States. Soon American settlers were moving to the West. They went for lots of different reasons. Some wanted land to farm while others went looking for gold, adventure, or an escape from religious persecution. They followed the trails that were made by early trappers and mountain men.

The West Timeline

May 1846 4-6
Mexican forces ambush two American companies and President Polk declares war on Mexico

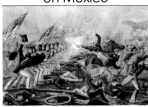

1846 4-6
Mormon Pioneers begin their westward migration

1846-1869 4-6
Peak years of the Oregon Trail

Jan 1848 4-6
Gold is discovered in California

Feb 1848 4-6
Treaty of Guadalupe Hidalgo is signed, ceding land of Texas, New Mexico and California to the U.S. from Mexico

Guadalupe Hidalgo
Gadsden Purchase

Sep 1850 4-6
California is admitted as a free state

1851 4-6
Indian Appropriations Act expands reservation system to the West

1854 4-6
13,000 Chinese immigrants enter the U.S. in California to work in gold mines and on the railroad

1860-61 4-6
Pony Express mail service

1862 4-6
Homestead Act gives 160 acres of free western land to anyone who is willing to live on and work the land

1862 4-6
Dakota War in Minnesota

1863 4-6
Gold discovered in Montana

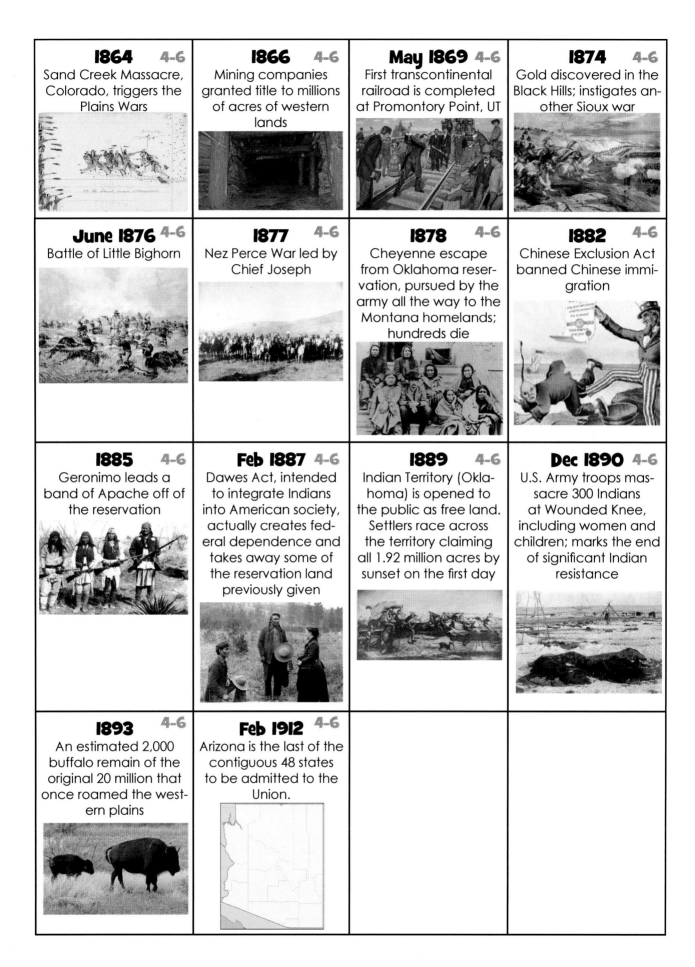

1864 4-6
Sand Creek Massacre, Colorado, triggers the Plains Wars

1866 4-6
Mining companies granted title to millions of acres of western lands

May 1869 4-6
First transcontinental railroad is completed at Promontory Point, UT

1874 4-6
Gold discovered in the Black Hills; instigates another Sioux war

June 1876 4-6
Battle of Little Bighorn

1877 4-6
Nez Perce War led by Chief Joseph

1878 4-6
Cheyenne escape from Oklahoma reservation, pursued by the army all the way to the Montana homelands; hundreds die

1882 4-6
Chinese Exclusion Act banned Chinese immigration

1885 4-6
Geronimo leads a band of Apache off of the reservation

Feb 1887 4-6
Dawes Act, intended to integrate Indians into American society, actually creates federal dependence and takes away some of the reservation land previously given

1889 4-6
Indian Territory (Oklahoma) is opened to the public as free land. Settlers race across the territory claiming all 1.92 million acres by sunset on the first day

Dec 1890 4-6
U.S. Army troops massacre 300 Indians at Wounded Knee, including women and children; marks the end of significant Indian resistance

1893 4-6
An estimated 2,000 buffalo remain of the original 20 million that once roamed the western plains

Feb 1912 4-6
Arizona is the last of the contiguous 48 states to be admitted to the Union.

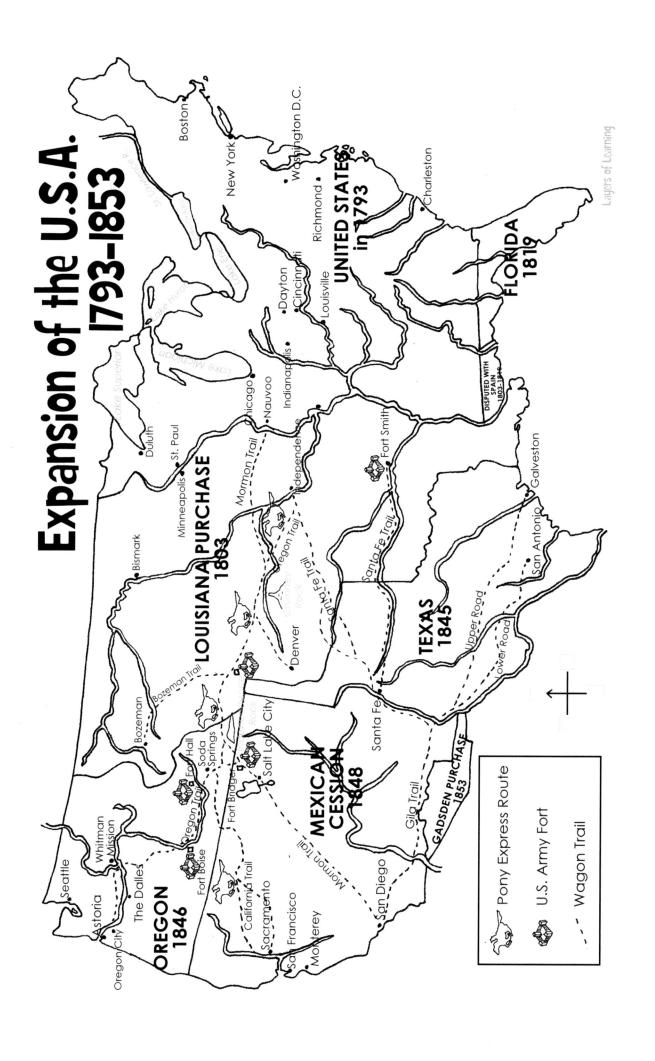

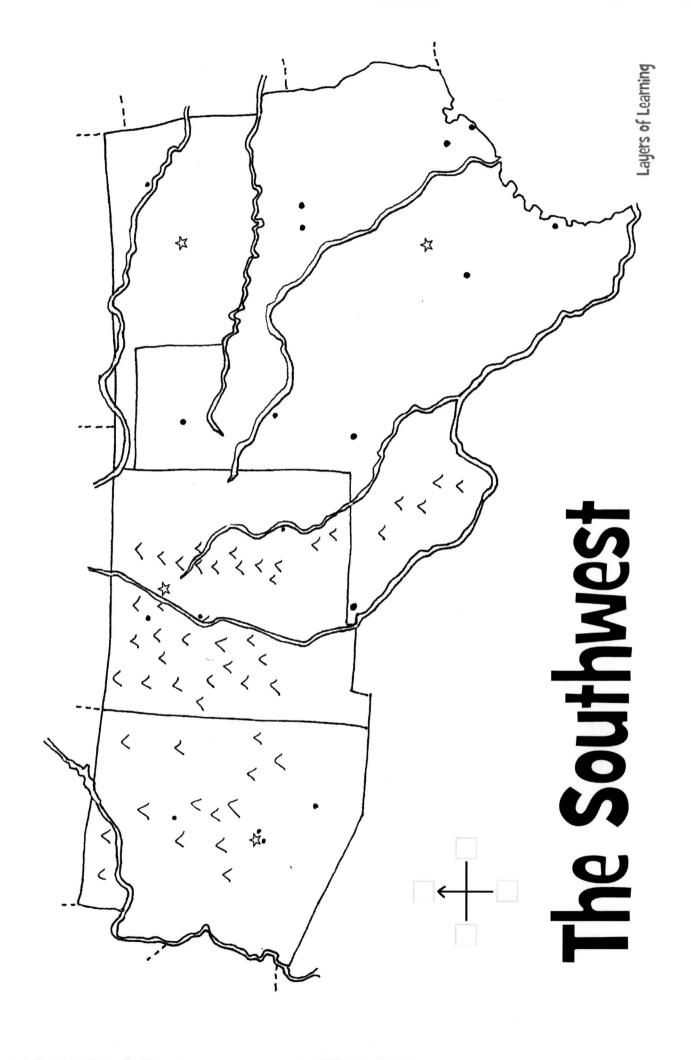

The Southwest

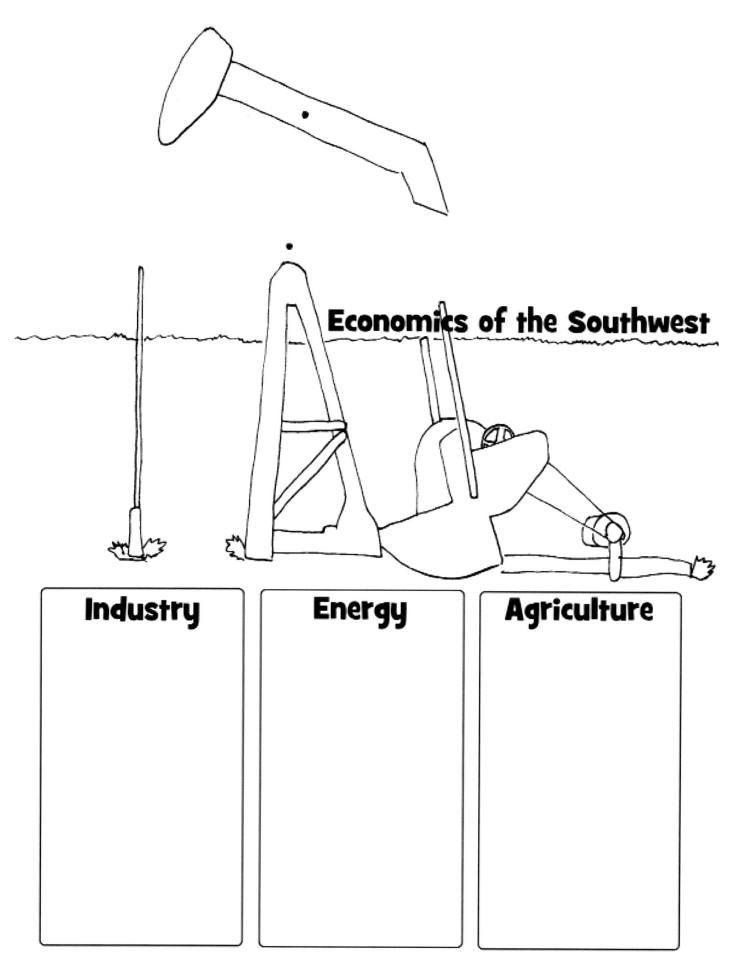

Economics of the Southwest

Industry

Energy

Agriculture

animals

history

symbols

plants

people

Structure of the Earth

Color each layer of the earth and then label the layers. Use the definitions below for help.

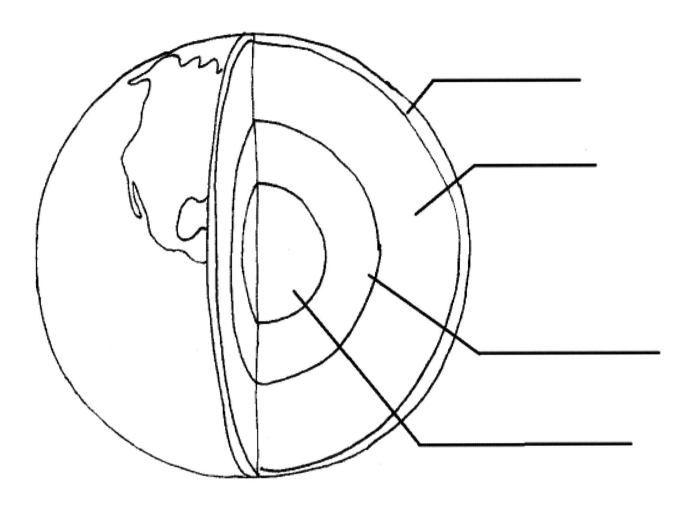

Crust: The outer layer of the earth. It is about 4 miles thick under the oceans and an average of 22 miles thick on the continents. The crust, together with the upper bit of the mantle, make up the lithosphere.

Mantle: The mantle is rocky, with molten rock in the zone between the mantle and the crust. It makes up most of the bulk of the earth at 1,800 miles thick. The minerals that surface from the mantle harden to become new crust.

Outer Core: The outer core is the liquid layer, made up of iron, nickel, and other unknown minerals. It is about 1,240 miles thick.

Inner Core: The inner core is thought to be solid and made of iron and nickel.

Earth's Layers

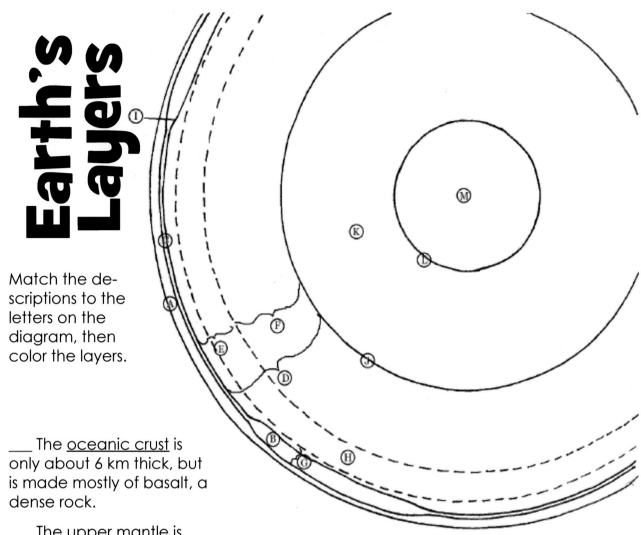

Match the descriptions to the letters on the diagram, then color the layers.

___ The <u>oceanic crust</u> is only about 6 km thick, but is made mostly of basalt, a dense rock.

___ The <u>upper mantle</u> is a very viscous melted or plastic rock.

___ The <u>Gutenberg Discontinuity</u> is the boundary between the mantle and outer core.

___ The outermost layer of the earth is completely gas. It is called the <u>atmosphere</u>.

___ The upper layer of the upper mantle is cooler and is solid rock. This, combined with the crust, is the <u>lithosphere</u>. The lithosphere is made mostly of silicates.

___ The <u>inner core</u> is also made of iron and nickel, but is under enough pressure to be mostly solid.

___ The <u>continental crust</u> is thick, an average of 35 km, but is made mostly of granite and is less dense than the oceanic crust.

___ The <u>mantle</u> is the thickest layer and makes up the bulk of the earth. It is divided into several regions.

___ The lower part of the upper mantle is called the <u>asthenosphere</u>.

___ The <u>Lehmann-Bullen Discontinuity</u> is the boundary between the inner and outer cores.

___ The <u>Mohorovicic Discontinuity</u> is the boundary between the mantle and the crust.

___ The <u>lower mantle</u> is very, very hot, but is under pressure, so it is more viscous than the upper mantle.

___ The <u>outer core</u> is made of iron and nickel and is molten metal.

Layers of Learning

Pissarro's Palette

The Fifer

About the Authors

Karen & Michelle . . .
Mothers, sisters, teachers, women who are passionate
about educating kids.
We are dedicated to lifelong learning.

Karen, a mother of four, who has homeschooled her kids for more than eight years with her husband, Bob, has a bachelor's degree in child development with an emphasis in education. She lives in Idaho, gardens, teaches piano, and plays an excruciating number of board games with her kids. Karen is our resident arts expert and English guru {most necessary as Michelle regularly and carelessly mangles the English language and occasionally steps over the bounds of polite society}.

Michelle and her husband, Cameron, have homeschooled their six boys for more than a decade. Michelle earned a bachelors in biology, making her the resident science expert, though she is mocked by her friends for being the Botanist with the Black Thumb of Death. She also is the go-to for history and government. She believes in staying up late, hot chocolate, and a no whining policy. We both pitch in on geography, in case you were wondering.

Visit our constantly updated blog for tons of free ideas,
free printables, and more cool stuff for sale:
www.Layers-of-Learning.com